Endorsements for *The Heart of Networking*

Ricky Steele's dedication as a volunteer is an example of how such a commitment to service can make a difference to communities and, indeed, to the nation.
—President Jimmy Carter

I have known Ricky Steele for many years through our mutual volunteering at different not-for-profit organizations in Atlanta. Ricky is one of Atlanta's great cheerleaders. His passion for our city and for serving the needs of our marginalized citizens is at the essence of what Atlanta is all about. As Mayor of the great city of Atlanta, I believe the message in Ricky's newest book focused on living the "Golden Rule through Servant Leadership" will inspire others to follow his example.

—Andre Dickens,
61st Mayor of Atlanta, Georgia

I've known Ricky Steele since the mid 80's. I was immediately drawn to Ricky because of his tremendous outgoing personality. Ricky is a large man and with his 'booming' voice he commands attention when he enters a room. Also, because of his warmth and generosity, you want to be around him.

I've always found Ricky to be one of the most genuine and sincere individuals I've ever met. I don't know if I've ever heard Ricky speak an unkind word about anyone. I would never describe his networking as work or in terms that made you feel there was disingenuousness about his interactions. I've always felt here is a man doing something he was called to do. He is a natural at connecting people no matter what their level or status.

—Eula Adams,
President First Data Corporation, Retired
Partner Deloitte

When I first met Ricky Steele in 1985, he said he had it in his heart to feed the hungry.

Luckily, I paid attention. The Food Bank had tried to engage the hospitality industry in our work with limited success. The outcome of Ricky's involvement was Atlanta's Table—a prepared and perishable food rescue program that quickly became a model for cities across the country.

Using the power of relationships, Ricky began a process that changed both the food bank and the restaurant & hospitality community. He is an exemplary example of how one person, a volunteer no less, can make a difference in the lives of millions of hungry people.

Ricky taught me how to engage and empower a network of people to make a difference. He has an uncanny ability to connect people with resources and ideas with passion. He combines the best of business know-how with faith in action. And for that I will be forever grateful.

—Bill Bolling,
Founder & (Retired) Executive Director
Atlanta Community Food Bank
Founder & Chairman
Food Well Alliance

Ricky Steele is a gift that just keeps on giving!!

His presence, his energy, his enthusiasm and his intellect are all wrapped up in a precious treasure chest that exudes love for others – way above himself – focused on the needs of others!!

His compassion for service and his expertise in networking create a powerhouse of effective communications and sustaining relationships!! Ricky Steele is the epitome of a servant leader, who graciously lives out those principles every day!!

Let's just list a few: listening, empathy, persuasion, commitment to the growth of people and building community!!! YES—this is Ricky Steele—a servant leader, who graciously gives his authentic love to all—every day by constantly looking to the needs of the people and asking himself how he can help them to solve problems!!!

Ricky is a leader, mentor, networking legend and I am so proud to call him friend!!!

—Ann Wilson Cramer,
Partner Coxe Curry
35-year IBM executive, Retired

When I think of what a TRUE community elder is, Ricky Steele is one of a handful of OG's who show that on a daily basis in Atlanta (and beyond, as I've come to learn, to no surprise).

As a representative of 'OutKast/'96 Olympics' Gen X youth of Atlanta, it has been a blessing to hear Ricky's stories filled with rare historic moments beautifully laced with sage wisdom that works whether you're analog and/or digital, lol!

It is an honor to place words on paper of your dopeness along with so many other giants, but even more of a blessing to call you my big homie! Looking forward to being a great griot like you and continuing to lead future generations in the way of Sensei Steele.

—Bem Joiner,
Co-Founder, Atlanta Influences Everything

I have watched Ricky Steele, use his power to bring people together, for good for decades.

He has impacted hundreds of thousands of people through his understanding and practices for how we can all be 'networked for good!'

I have never met anyone as good as Ricky at creating relationships in pursuit of purpose.

In this book, he shares his powers and idea so that we can all extend our connections and cultivate stronger communities.

—Michelle Nunn,
CARE USA
President and CEO

I first heard from my daughter, Michelle, about Ricky Steele and his idea for a new community outreach concept to involve visiting conventioneers in Atlanta service projects. My response: Noble theory, but it won't work.

Little did I know of Ricky's connections, energy, and determination. Through the power of his network and the partnership with Hands on Atlanta, great things have occurred. I have never been more pleased to say, 'I was wrong,' and to be reminded again of Margaret Mead's quote, 'Never doubt that a small group of thoughtful, committed citizens can change the world—indeed, it is the only thing that ever has.'

—Sam Nunn,
CEO, Nuclear Threat Initiative
Former United States Senator

Ricky Steele is a one-of-a-kind networker, genuine friend and spiritually guided entrepreneur. Through his unique and serendipitous experiences, Ricky has created a 'must read' chronicle of unique chapters in his life that he generously shares with others.

Whether highlighting his successes or lessons learned from his business obstacles, Ricky once again presents a unique perspective on the importance of friendship, networking and doing the right thing. This is a book to keep on your bookshelf and to consult whenever you need sage guidance from a true friend.

—John C. Yates,
Morris, Manning & Martin, LLP

Working with Ricky Steele was an adventure in laughter, humility and love.

No two days were ever the same - which is saying something at a staid accounting firm like PricewaterhouseCoopers! - except for the fundamentals of decency and dignity with which Ricky accorded everyone he encountered.

Ricky's sense of humor is second to none and it made him irresistible to all, from CEOs to the clerks behind the Krispy Kreme counter. At the heights of the dot.com boom in 2000, there was no lack of ego in tech startups' founders. They all, however, sought out Ricky, who never once wavered in how he treated everyone...with a joke to start, an answer or referral to someone with the answer, a thoughtful commitment to make helpful introductions and connections, but always, also, a caring heart for that person as a person, not just as a "source of revenue" to our employer.

Not a week went by that I didn't receive a phone call or get stopped at a meeting from those same CEO's who all wanted to know the same thing. "Is he for real?" They just couldn't get over that, all in one package, someone could be that that genuinely funny, helpful and caring.

I assured each of them that, with Ricky, what they saw and/or heard, was who he actually was. No guile or ulterior motives.

Completely transparent.

I learned more from Ricky about servant leadership, how to really live out my Christian faith, and the irresistible power of a heart for others, than I have in a lifetime of sermons. Yes, he IS the "real deal" and you'd be wise to incorporate his suggestions into making a better you!

—Susan O'Dwyer,
Retired PricewaterhouseCoopers

Ricky Steele has been associated with Leadership Atlanta for over thirty-five years, and his love and enthusiasm for the organization has never faltered.

He has been involved in so many ways. Ricky has served on the Board of Trustees and chaired numerous programs and events. He has directed traffic for us in ninety-degree weather, and, perhaps most importantly, he has spoken to multiple Leadership Atlanta classes about his passion—networking. Ricky has so much to say and so many stories to tell, and he does it well.

Atlanta is a better place because of Ricky Steele. His passion for people and networking has been demonstrated throughout Atlanta. Ricky Steele's gifts are his desire and ability to truly connect with people from all walks of life.

He has mastered both walking with the masses 'while maintaining virtue' and walking with kings 'without losing the common touch.' As a master networker, his perspective on networking is compelling.

—Pat Upshaw-Monteith,
President and CEO, Leadership Atlanta

The Heart
of Networking

BOOKLOGIX
Alpharetta, GA

The Heart of Networking
Third Edition

ISBN: 978-1-6653-0512-9 – Hardcover
ISBN: 978-1-6653-0513-6 – Epub

Library of Congress Control Number: 2022918582

♾This paper meets the requirements of ANSI/NISO Z39.48-1992 (Permanence of Paper)

1 1 1 1 2 2

The Heart
of Networking

Third Edition

■

Ricky Steele

Contents

Preface

THANK YOU FOR PICKING UP THIS BOOK TO READ. It was first published shortly after my seventieth birthday. This is my last book on networking, the trait and trade I have been practicing since I was nine or ten years old, having watched my father, who was a great networker three or four decades before anyone ever heard the word. As I said, this is my last book on the subject, so it is longer, deeper, and a lot rougher around the edges than the first two editions. For the first time, I share stories using the names of the folks involved, with their permission.

There are stories about parts of my life that I have never shared with anyone other than family and very close friends, and some may think they have nothing to do with networking, but they would be wrong. Those who have read the first or second edition will recognize many points and stories I shared in the earlier books, because they are at the "heart" of my networking experiences and well worth sharing again.

My goal has remained constant through the three editions. It is to equip you to change your world and perhaps even the world we all live in.

You are amazing, and you have powers I have never had or will ever possess. The only thing stopping you from changing the world is fear of failure. At the very least, my life story should show you that failure is okay. No one is perfect. We all fail. That's fine. What you cannot let yourself do is quit. I am a lifelong failure. I have been thrown from far too many horses along the way because of choices I made as a young child, student, husband, father, brother to my siblings, friend, business owner, employee, and volunteer. Well, the list goes on and on. I have learned over many broken bones that the only way to move forward from failure is to get back on the horse and continue the journey. Call this a "failure to quit." It has allowed me to experience some amazing highs in most of the areas in which I failed earlier in life. Sadly, I said most, not all. I pray that, over time, I will reverse previous failures into great moments of restoration. At seventy, I don't know if I have six months or twenty years to remain on this journey, but I give you my word, I will keep getting back on that horse until God calls me to join Him for eternity.

We are taught that, in business, nothing happens until money changes hands. You may be proud of yourself for adding twenty-two new names to your database of contacts this week. Your boss may even think this is a great thing. Nevertheless, in the end, if you are unable to "convert" a certain number of your prospects into sales, someone else will soon be sitting at your desk.

I understand and live with this truth. I have had the privilege of working in many industries, including the concessions operation of a Double-A professional baseball team, the transportation and hospitality business, and travel magazine publishing. I have also served as a director for the world's largest accounting firm, PricewaterhouseCoopers LLP; a Division President for Cox Enterprises; a Client Partner with the world's largest executive search firm, Korn/Ferry International; as well as the CEO of ten different start-up companies in six different industries.

Today, I am in the process of winding down my career. I have been officially working since 1964, when I received my first W-2 as the bat boy for the Columbus Yankees Double A baseball team fifty-eight years ago as I write these words. After taking roughly two years off to deal with the death of our thirty-three-year-old son, Andrew, I joined Talent 360 Solutions, a boutique staffing agency led by two smart, hardworking young men, Kevin Raxter and Matt Fox. Matt went to school with my oldest son, and at one point I tried to hire Matt for my staffing firm. The first lesson I share is to always treat everyone with great respect because the person you interview today just may interview you a few years later.

Am I retiring with the publication of this book? No, my wife will not allow me to be home on a full-time basis, and those who know me well understand her reasons very well. I will continue at Talent 360

Solutions for as long as they will have me because we are having fun, growing the business, and it gives me the opportunity to continue serving my old friends, who are also my clients. It also gives my wife and me the ability to share financial support with the not-for-profit organizations we believe are making the world a more equitable place for all of God's children.

The bottom-line truth concerning the need to make sales has applied in each of these many diverse venues, but it is neither the only truth nor the most important one. The vision all too many companies have for their "long-term" success looks no farther than the next quarter. And this shortsightedness, common though it is, is a terrible mistake. Individual sales happen or fail to happen, but the kinds of relationships that dependably produce one sale after another, quarter after quarter, year after year, are nurtured for months, if not years before a single dollar ever changes hands. All too few employers, let alone employees, have the patient stomach for that kind of relationship building. If you are among the few who are willing to make the commitment of time and effort necessary to conduct genuine, effective networking, this book is for you. If, however, you are among the nervous majority, I am sure you can find books with titles like *How to Close a Piece of Business by 5:00 P.M. Today.*

The Heart of Networking operates on a different timetable.

To begin with, most people think of networking as boozing and schmoozing in an attempt to make someone like you enough to do business with you. Nothing could be further from the truth.

You see, a successful networker understands and believes that his or her first mission has nothing to do with selling anything to anybody. The mission of networking is to build relationships, which may or may not lead directly to business one day. Build enough relationships, and you have created an environment favorable to your success. Instead of scrambling for a sale on Tuesday and another on Friday, you will have enabled a universe of potential customers and clients, who, collectively, produce a steady stream of sales for which you need not scramble. Good thing, too. Because if you are networking the right way, you're working so hard at creating relationships that you don't have any spare time for all that scrambling. Leave that to others, to those with enough frenetic energy to reinvent the wheel each time they want to make a sale. You're more interested in setting things up for the long term, so the sales take care of themselves.

Sales and marketing executives today more than ever feel the pressure to produce revenue. It is natural to respond by scrambling for this or that sale. Our goal, however, should be to create a relationship with our prospects, regardless of whether they buy today or not. If you can build a relationship and earn the trust of your prospects, it is more than likely you will either do business with them directly or they will become a source of referrals for you. It may not happen today. It may not happen tomorrow. But it will happen. And if your network is sufficiently wide and deep, sales will be far more plentiful than what you could ever hope to produce in a professional life devoted to scrambling.

How do I know? I have seen and experienced it myself too many times to count. As someone who has worked in many different industries, I have current clients with whom I worked during multiple past careers. We have a relationship, and they trust me. They really do not care what products or services I might be representing, if they have a need in that area, they make a choice to call me first.

I hate cold calling and to be honest, I like to brag that I have not made a cold call since Richard Nixon was president, but since too many of you are not old enough to remember President Nixon, I will say that I have not made a cold call since President Clinton was in office.

Although these boasts may not be entirely accurate, I make far fewer cold calls than anyone I know because I built life-changing, long-lasting relationships in the 1970s and every decade since. These have produced a network of friends. I also share from time to time that I am the only salesperson I know who does not have any clients. I have only friends and friends of friends who choose to do business with me because of our relationship.

As hard as it may be to exercise the patience networking requires, it is even harder to practice another aspect of building successful relationships. Sometimes we must walk away from business when our product or service is not the best fit. If you turn down business *and* tell your prospect the reasons why, you will lose a sale today, but you will gain a friend, whose influence may win you sale after sale after sale a little later. The next time this prospect has a need that is even close to your sweet spot, you're sure to get the call. Why? First, he trusts you to do an excellent job, and second, if you don't have the right solution, he can count on your honesty to tell him so and your friendship to point him in a productive direction. Beyond this, you will also benefit from the many referrals he will give you. The beauty of a network is that you are not the only node from which the lines of relationship emanate. Each of your contacts is a node on your network, and from each node lines run to others.

It is a sad fact that many people believe the best way to tell if a salesperson is lying is to see if his lips are moving. Even sadder is the reason behind this stereotype. Many, many people, out for the quick buck, are unhampered by scruples. They have harmed decent salespeople everywhere. If you consistently demonstrate that you do what you say you are going to do and deliver what you say you are going to deliver, then you will be perceived as that most valuable of human beings: the exception. People will *want* to know you.

It is much more likely that you will make sales among a group of people who want to know you than among a group of people who want to avoid you like the plague. But don't kid yourself. This is still hard work. Once you win a customer, you own him or her. Now, that "ownership" gives you absolutely no rights, but it does entail a lot of responsibilities. You must maintain the relationship. If you or your company fall short on anything promised, you can't afford to let your customer be the one to discover the fact for himself. Pick up the phone or, better yet, go to the customer's office, even if it requires hopping a plane to do so. Explain the situation without blaming your assistant or the folks in shipping or quality control. Once everything is out on the table, ask for forgiveness, and, most important of all, tell the client what you are going to do to correct the problem.

I have been humbled by the look of amazement on a client's face when I take ownership of a problem and promise to make it right. When was the last time someone you do business with treated you this way? For myself, I don't remember experiencing this type of service but once or twice in my entire life, yet I know it is how I would *like* to be treated all of the time, and because I know that it is how *I* would like to be treated, it is the way I treat my clients and customers. Nothing new here, of course: This is the Golden Rule.

It is the heart of networking.

Let's get started.

—Ricky Steele

1

■

Networking Man

IN 1979, I MOVED TO ATLANTA FROM WHERE I GREW UP, Columbus, Georgia, a hundred miles to the southwest and just about a whole universe away. Columbus was a town of about 160,000 back then and was known to a few people for a few things: textiles and small manufacturing, plus proximity to the army's Fort Benning. Columbus had given birth to Blues great Ma Rainey and novelist Carson McCullers, who wrote *Ballad of the Sad Café*. Both were long dead by 1979. Some might say it was a redneck town, but that word's become a stereotype with too many ugly connotations, so let's agree it was pretty much blue collar, by which I mean hardworking and honorable, but hardly the most likely place to do what I did early the year before I moved.

I probably should have figured out from the get-go that blue denim is not a great fit with chauffeured chrome and shiny black sheet metal—even if our corporate motto was "If we can get it cranked, we will pick you up." After nearly two years of losing money, we closed our office in Columbus, and I moved to Atlanta, either to make the business work or go bankrupt in the big city. This wasn't do-or-die bravado but the way I really felt at that point. Truth to tell, of the two possibilities, make it work or go bankrupt, I thought the second a lot more likely, and Atlanta had the big advantage of not being Columbus, where declaring bankruptcy would be far more embarrassing to my family and me.

The Boarding Gate

At the time, metro Atlanta had an urban and suburban population of nearly three million. (Today it's more than six spread over thirty-one counties.) I assumed that a sizable portion of that three mil was sure to want limo service more than once in a while. The only problem was that I didn't know five people in the city or its suburbs who were not my relatives. I *did* know that the very first thing I had to do was go to Hartsfield Airport (today Hartsfield-Jackson International Airport) and apply for limousine and chauffeur permits. To say I was intimidated qualifies as one of the great understatements of all time. Just because you happen to be six-three and weigh well north of two hundred pounds doesn't mean you're automatically the most confident person treading the earth. The fact is that meeting people for the first time had been a struggle for me all my life. And still is.

Okay. I'm giving myself a little harder time than I deserve. I did not drive into Atlanta in complete darkness. I had read enough beforehand to decide that a good person to try to meet was Mr. George Berry, at the time the city's Commissioner of Aviation. At the airport, I filled out the necessary forms, paid the required fees, called on the designated clerk, and secured the permits. I could now be on my way, but instead I decided to call on Mr. Berry—personally. I had no reason to believe that he would want to see me. Technically, I had no further business with his department, let alone with him, the top man. On the other hand, the permits were under his jurisdiction, and I had as much right as anyone to ask for a meeting. So, on my very first visit to the airport, I summoned up the courage to drop by his office. I asked the receptionist if Mr. Berry was in.

"Do you have an appointment?" she asked in return.

The word *receptionist* is one of the most blatant misnomers in the English language. It implies that the function of this person is to *receive* callers when, in truth, his or her real function is to *screen* callers and, whenever possible, repel their entry. On most people, the question, "Do you have an appointment?" casts a kind of magic spell, instantly making the would-be caller disappear. But, of course, "most people" would never have tried making a go of a limo company in a little southwest Georgia city. So, I didn't disappear, but instead smiled and replied to her: "No, but I am new in town, and I have heard a lot about Mr. Berry, and I just wanted to say hello."

As it turned out, I had some magic words of my own, and they have rarely failed me. Virtually everyone who comes calling on people who occupy the kind of position George Berry held want something. Hence the need for a so-called receptionist to bar the way. However, all I told her I wanted was to "say hello," which is no great demand on anyone, and, even more important, I came not so much *asking* as *offering*. What I offered was the respect born of my sense of Mr. Berry's importance. "I have heard a lot about" him, I said.

It worked. Without an appointment and within minutes, Mr. Berry came out. We shook hands, I told him that he was well known even in my corner of the state, and I thanked him for selling me the permits.

At that time, Mr. Berry was overseeing a $500 million-dollar construction project for the city's new Hartsfield, and he was also dealing daily with the major airlines on matters involving additional millions of dollars. I'm sure he was taken aback by being thanked for selling me two permits at a total cost of some $300. What I had done—thanking him personally—was no great achievement, of course, but it was extraordinary, nevertheless. And, for that reason, it marked me as extraordinary—at least in the eyes of George Berry. He told me that I was welcome and invited me to come back anytime.

I did.

Over the next months and years, Mr. Berry became George, and he introduced me to many great folks on his staff, who not only helped me learn the ins and outs of Atlanta's airport but became great friends. Later, George left the airport to become the Director of Industry, Trade, and Tourism for the state of Georgia. He gave me the opportunity to bid on and win the rights to the publication of the official travel guide for Georgia. Thanks also to George, I had the pleasure of coordinating transportation for the Southern Governors Conference in the mid-1980s, held at the Cloister in Sea Island, Georgia. During the conference, I met people as diverse as Ray Charles and Governor Bill and Mrs. Hillary Clinton from Arkansas. By this time, I was very well established in the Atlanta-area limousine business and hospitality industry.

Did I owe it all to George Berry?

No. But if I hadn't worked up the courage to talk to him that first day at the airport, I'm reasonably sure I would have ended up declaring bankruptcy in Atlanta and returning to Columbus, tail between my legs. Mr. George Berry passed in 2019, but I will never forget him and it was an honor to know him.

Just Meeting People

Encouraged in part by the generous, open way in which George Berry had received me, I began more consciously and deliberately to "network"—though I wouldn't have called it that back then. It was just "meeting people," and you can never meet too many people, because the larger your network, the greater your capacity to grow. How big do you want to become?

Well, in 1979, for me, there was just one *positive* direction to go, which was to become bigger than I was. So, I started asking around and was told by more than one person that a great place to learn more about the limousine and hospitality industries was the Atlanta Convention and Visitors Bureau. I called the ACVB office, asked about joining, then drove to the bureau and wrote a $265 check—which, at the time, may or may not have been good. This notwithstanding, I delivered the check into the hands of Mr. W. B. Baldwin III, the bureau's vice president of marketing and membership. With a smile, he invited me into his office.

The moment, I realized, was *now*.

Again, I was hardly brimming with confidence; believe me, that's just not in my nature. In fact, I was shaking in my boots when I asked Mr. Baldwin to tell me what I could do to learn more about the hospitality business and how I could get more involved in the work of the bureau.

Why was I so nervous? What was I afraid of? Rejection? I hadn't burst through his door demanding to be helped and insisting on answers. I had just handed the man a check—however dubious its value. I had *given* something. The situation of giving is not conducive to rejection, but even I didn't expect the bounty I was about to receive. Seeking no more than information, I was handed an offer. Mr. Baldwin said there just happened to be a membership reception that very afternoon, and he offered me an invitation.

He didn't have to ask me twice. I attended, I listened, and I learned. When everyone was offered an opportunity to join one of the bureau's committees, I bit. My hope was that, at the very least, joining would gain me introductions to other committee members. Now, I heard a rumor buzzing about the room that the absolute *worst* committee to join was the Membership Committee, because you were expected to hoof it, soliciting memberships. The *worst* committee? Sure, it called for some unpaid work, but, for my purposes, it was the committee with the most bang for the buck. Not only would it give me the opportunity to meet my fellow committee members, but I would also be meeting as many other industry movers and shakers as I could reach.

A lot of small business owners wince and groan when they talk about their early days and how they struggled through a slow and perilous start-up. Well, my start-up was slow and perilous enough, I assure you, but I used the otherwise dead time to my advantage. I devoted it to selling memberships, and I ended up selling more than any volunteer in the history of the bureau and almost as many as the ACVB's full-time salesperson. Not much more time passed before Mr. Baldwin became plain old "W. B."

I had nothing to prove, and even after I broke sales records, I kept right on selling. I knew that you can never meet too many people. For me, selling has always been about meeting new people, and selling memberships to the ACVB was meeting new people in exactly the industry I was trying to enter. But all my sales soon caught the attention of Mr. William Cambre, the executive vice president of the bureau's Board of Directors for Membership. That was his volunteer position. His *paying* job was senior officer for Eastern Airlines in the Southeast, and his headquarters was Atlanta. Mr. Cambre called me one day to invite me to his office for a cup of coffee.

"Ricky," he said to me as I made myself comfortable, "I like you. I have been watching you for some time. You are always trying to be helpful, and you seem to go out of your way for the bureau. I would like to help *you* over the next few years. Would that be okay with you?"

At that moment, I was quite willing to name my first two children after him and wash his car every day for the foreseeable future. Soon, I found myself appointed to the board of the Atlanta Convention and Visitors Bureau—an eventuality that more than mildly upset several older and more established transportation company owners, who had been trying unsuccessfully for years to get on the board.

Had I, like these others, *tried* to get on the board? No. Had I asked Mr. Cambre for the position? No. Had I even asked to meet him? Again, no.

What I *had* done was to grow a network, nourishing it by always offering much more than I asked for. Funny thing is that, as much as I gave, I always received much more in return. I *gave* the bureau a lot of memberships, but I *received* scores and scores of key business contacts and, finally, a coveted seat on the board of directors. Not by demanding or even asking did I get these things, but by giving. That is the essence of networking.

Over the ten years or so following my appointment to the ACVB board, I had experiences that someone with my background and education had no right to imagine, let alone seek. For several years running, I was invited on every Eastern Airlines inaugural flight out of Atlanta, always in company with executives from the chamber of commerce, local corporations, and government officials—people whose decisions would build my business. My wife, Beth, and I had the privilege of going to London with one of my heroes, civil rights leader and United Nations ambassador Andrew Young, who was Atlanta's mayor at the time. In company with then Lieutenant Governor Zell Miller and Shirley Franklin (at the time a deputy director in Mayor Young's administration and, later, mayor of Atlanta), we sold Atlanta as a great convention city, talking with meeting planners, travels agents, and corporate officers in New York, Washington, and Chicago, as well as London.

I could never have dreamed, let alone planned what happened as a result of Mr. Cambre's kindness. Years later, I attended Mr. Cambre's funeral and sat in a church full of his other convention industry friends.

By this time, I had heard stories about the many others to whom he had offered himself as a mentor, and I realized that he had done in a big way what I was doing in a smaller way. He had, every day, given without expecting anything in return. That was the way he lived. I myself had learned that something given to another in the expectation of quid quo pro is no gift at all, but, at best, an installment on a future purchase or, at worst, a bribe. However, give without the expectation of return, and, over the long term, there is almost always a return, nevertheless. Often, it is a blessing out of all proportion to what you have given.

The Power of Networking

They say it's better to be lucky than smart. I've built several businesses without a prodigious helping of either luck or smarts. I did it by networking. I've just told you about some of the results. According to the dictionary, a *network* is "a group, or system, of interconnected individuals." In other words, it's people relating to other people. Here's a blinding glimpse of the obvious: Without people, networking cannot and will not happen.

But maybe it's not quite so obvious. We live in a day of e-mails, instant messages, 24/7 Internet connectivity, iPhones, social networking tools, and Zoom/Skype/Teams calls. Common sense says these all save a lot of time, expense, and trouble. This was especially true when Covid-19 reduced both desirability and feasibility of travel. But, Covid or no Covid, none of us particularly enjoys trekking to the airport to begin a forty-five-minute flight with a two-hour odyssey through security before we even reach the gate. Using digital technology to avoid physical travel seems the height of common sense.

But maybe what we need is a little *un*common sense. Serious networking takes more than a call, text, e-mail, or even a quick Zoom. As little as these cost, they're not cost-effective if they don't produce results. Eyeball to eyeball is where I get my greatest satisfaction. I enjoy feeling somebody's hand in mine as we make eye contact, whether I'm greeting an old associate, client, or friend or meeting for the first time a potential any one of these.

Networking in the Time of Covid

As I am writing this in late summer of 2022, Covid-19 and its variants have been with us for over two and a half years. Almost 8 million people across the world and more than a million in the United States alone have died. Nobody knows for sure how many millions more have been ill but survived and recovered.

Covid had changed the world and certainly changed the way I do what I do. This may be the new normal for a long time or even forever. If that turns out to be the case, I am sad for us all and, I admit it, especially for myself because I am passionate about people. At this point in my life, I don't golf, fish, play tennis, hunt, or do many of the other things some people find fun, exciting, and fulfilling. Today, my focus is my faith, my family, my friends, colleagues, a great meal with a good bottle of wine, laughter, and live music.

Every one of these things revolves around one central component: other people. God created a very diverse and multi-cultured population among which there are many folks to meet, share fellowship with, extend help to, receive help from, and just spend time together in harmony. In March of 2020 when Cov-19 began the lockdown, it modified or halted outright every behavior we had lived with for untold generations.

Personally, I lost weight because I no longer scheduled three breakfast meetings, a lunch or two, a reception and/or dinner four days a week. Far more precious than the few pounds I lost was the ability to shake a hand, hug another human being, share a kiss on the cheek with folks who are family by birth and those who are family by our faith, belief system, mutual love of others, and everything that revolves around the joy of sharing and receiving love.

When the pandemic hit, I was just starting a new job with Talent 360 Solutions. I already had my prospect list filled with over fifty names, and not a single one of them was a stranger.

These were people I had done business with before. We volunteered together, we knew each other's families, and we would do most anything to help one another. I wanted to share a meal and fellowship face to face with all fifty over the following four or five months as we had done so many times in the past. For me, all of that stopped as of March 13, 2020.

What did I do?

I was ticked. I was sad. I knew that life was not going to be the same for who knew how long. I first thought that the lockdown would last two or three months. It turned out to be twelve months, eighteen months, and, as I write this after 2.5 years, things are still not back to pre-Covid "normal."

Like so many others, with the Covid-19 vaccine roll out, after my two doses and the booster, I began the process of inviting people who were also vaccinated to meet at restaurants with outside seating, which worked great in good weather, terrible in bad weather—unless the venue was prepared. I began finding places that had *covered* outdoor seating, with huge fans for warm weather and heaters for cold weather. Still, I have been able to share face-to-face meals outside my home only at a fraction of my pre-Covid rate.

On the other hand, I have spoken on the telephone more than I ever have. Add to that the Skyping, Zooming, Teams Live meetings, and meeting on other video platforms. Compared to a face-to-face meeting, the best I can say is that video conferencing is pretty horrible. Compared to a plain old phone call, however, it is a miracle of God.

Over the last Covid-shrouded year, I have met with hundreds of people one on one, on small conference calls, attended Leadership Atlanta, TechBridge, Conscious Capitalism, Atlanta Community Food Bank, Outstanding Atlanta, and a number of other business or not-for-profit meetings online. To be able to see these dear friends and to watch them smile, laugh, and share other expressions is a gift that I consider extraordinary. The beauty of these calls is not just the educational value of the program or the discussion, but the opportunity to interact with the other viewers. I have met new friends and caught up with dear friends in the chat section of the video page. Some organizations block the chat feature and even block the names of the other participants. I understand the desire to reduce what some consider distraction, but I hope they draw the line at discouraging the free interchange of ideas—even if some of the ideas are off-topic.

During the pandemic, I do my best to be much more focused on what I can do for others. Everyone is stressed, many people are lonely, and many people are between jobs or are desperate to make new sales. On a regular basis, I post on Facebook, LinkedIn, and Twitter that I have some free time and if there is anything I may do for anyone in my network, I am open. I give my personal email and cell phone number. This gesture has not produced a single truly life-changing moment that I am aware of, but it did produce many "Likes," "Loves," and a number of "Thank you very much, I needed that" responses. I also am posting a lot more Likes, Loves, Agrees, and Shares while also adding many more comments on posts made by others in my network. Such responses don't cost a dime, and if they lift up the person and their ideas and views, I think I've done some important work. Because I have an active social media network of over fifteen thousand, between LinkedIn, Facebook, and Twitter, many people have told me that by my sharing their post, it went viral, and they have been exposed to hundreds of new contacts.

I look for folks, often on Facebook, who share a painful situation related to Covid-19 illness for themselves or their family, including a few who lost someone from Covid-19. I believe empathy is a very precious commodity always but never more than in these hard days.

It's not *all* bad. During the pandemic, I have found it easier to make LinkedIn connections. Everyone is online all the time. Over the past several months, I have added hundreds of new contacts at companies where I do business or would like to do business. I spend time doing my research and then ask the person to Link with a reason or question as to why we might be a good match. In the initial contact or on your last contact before they block you, never ever ask for business or a job. To do so is an opportunity killer, big time. You are there to start a relationship, nothing more and nothing less, even if an aspiration to something more concrete is in the back of your mind.

Precisely because everyone is online 24/7, the time has never been better time to send a handwritten note to a home address. If you don't have that address, send an email or text to tell them that you have something you want to send them and, with offices half-staffed, would it be easier to send it to their home? If you know them well enough and they would think it humorous, you might add, "I promise not to ever visit your home unless specifically asked."

Networking is a conscious and disciplined extension of what comes naturally. I told you that I'm shy, that I have a hard time meeting new people. And it's true. Yet, nevertheless, I realize that I've been networking for as long as I can remember. I learned from the greatest networker I have personally known: my dad. I remember, when I was eight or nine, going to his office almost every Saturday and sometimes in the middle of the week after school. I'm sure that at least some of these visits were my mother's idea, sparked by a phone call to the effect that if dad didn't come and get me, Mom was going to kill me. Regardless of the reason for my being with him, I watched Dad at his office and in business meetings all around Columbus.

This is what I saw: He never failed to stick out his hand and greet anyone who approached him. The mayor or the restaurant waiter, it made no difference. I will never forget how the minister at my father's funeral in February of 2002 spent a lot of time talking about my father's hands. He said the first time he shook hands with Dad, he was frightened. He was unsure if he would ever see his own hand again. He worried that if my father, as the chairman of our church's board of trustees, got really upset with him, he did not fear losing his ministerial job, he feared losing his life. He then turned to say, in his twenty-plus years of knowing my father, he had never once seen his hands balled into a fist. Dad's hands were always open to share with others whatever he had. His hands were also open to quickly receive help from others when it was offered.

I learned from this. A fist shuts off all meaningful conversation. We are closed to fresh ideas, emotions, and wisdom. Unwilling to share the same with others, we are as dead as the Dead Sea, and we die lonely deaths daily. Mahatma Gandhi said: "You cannot shake hands with a clenched fist." As a person who makes a living by shaking hands, it is a lesson that I was blessed to learn early in life."

I thank God for what I learned from Dad—daily. Every day, at home, our telephone rang at all hours of the day and night, conveying the voices of people asking dad for help or advice. Dad always gave both, and, by doing so, built a network, which I then saw him use to assemble teams of people to accomplish great things. Dad was the moving force behind a movement to lure minor league baseball back to Columbus in 1964 after the town had gone five long years without a team. Once he had the team here, he used it to help our city change. The fact that minor league teams were filled with young athletes both black and white could be a serious problem in a time when much of the South was struggling with—and often struggling against—racial integration. Sometimes the team would play away-games in cities with segregated hotels. The usual practice was for a team to make two stops after a game, dropping off the white players at one hotel and the black players at another.

Dad had a rule he would not break. The players on the Columbus team always stayed together in the same hotel. Usually, this meant that all the players, black and white, stayed in the "worst" hotel the town had to offer, because only the "worst" hotels were integrated. My dad thought these were the *best*. He himself was a partner in the largest and finest hotel in Columbus, The Ralston Hotel. It was the hotel that hosted most business and civic clubs like the Rotary, Kiwanis, Exchange Club as well as the place where many wedding receptions and City of Columbus government receptions were most often held. It was always dad's policy to allow all ballplayers from visiting teams, black and white, to stay together. This was a courageous stance in 1964 and 1965, and many times our phone rang not with the usual requests for help and advice, but with curses and threats. A local sign painter applied his trade to further his views on race relations. His sign shop was on the way to the ballpark, and we were always curious, uncomfortable, and ultimately proud to see what sign the owner would display next in his shop window about our dad. "Dick Steele is a nigger lover and is ruining our city" is one I remember most clearly because it stayed on display for week after week.

A few years ago, former Columbus Yankee, later a great New York Yankee and Detroit Tiger pitcher, Mr. Fritz Peterson, posted a tribute to my father on Facebook on the Martin Luther King, Jr. holiday. Mr. Peterson said: "Baseball is full of heroes like Mr. Steele, some not as well-known as Branch Rickey and Jackie Robinson, but still hugely important people in baseball history. If the Hall of Fame had a Civil Rights wing, Dick Steele would have earned a place there."

Networking? My father taught me everything I know about the brotherhood of man, which, whatever else it is, is at the very heart of networking.

Giving and Getting

Dad and his investors lost money almost every year on the baseball franchise until they finally sold it in 1984 or 1985. Long before this, year after year, I asked dad why he didn't unload the franchise or just close it down.

"Son, we don't lose much on the team," he'd say. "This is for our community. Every night, thousands of men, women, and children come to the ballpark for inexpensive recreation. You cannot always be a taker; you have to give back to your community."

That word "community," I learned, is the key. It can mean your town, your neighborhood, your nation, your company, your industry, or your family, but whatever it means, it always includes *you*. In the long run, what you give to your community you give to yourself by building and improving the reality in which you live and work. In the long run, what you give to the community comes back to you, magnified. I know my father made the world a better place, and he made me a better person. As the *community* of Columbus was his network in space—that space being a little chunk of southwestern Georgia—*I* am part of his network in time. What he gave years ago still lives through me today, and I have attempted to pass it on to my children. Each of them is active in the continued struggle for civil and human rights, which makes me quite proud. This business of networking is much bigger than any single firm or industry. It's a way of working and a way of living, and it can make the way you live and work far more successful and rewarding than you ever dreamed.

2

■

Getting Reality Ready for You

IMAGINE, SAY, TEN PEOPLE IN A ROOM. You make the following statement to them: "The goal of education is to get our children ready for reality." Then you ask: "Who agrees? Show of hands."

I'll lay any wager you please that ten hands will wave in the air. And ten people will be wrong.

If they weren't, folks like my dad would still be hunting up lodgings for their integrated ball teams. A segregated South was the reality most people had been educated to accept since before the Civil War. For that matter, if those ten imaginary people in that hypothetical room were right, I suppose we'd have no teams and no hotels and no baseball but would still be tracing pictures of our hands on the walls of caves. The Stone Age, after all, was the reality for which generation after generation had been made ready and therefore accepted without question.

No, the true goal of education has never been to ready us for reality, but to prepare us to make reality ready for whatever innovations advance this great collective enterprise called civilization.

Like education, networking is not about "accepting" reality. It is about wading into reality and getting it into a shape that enables you to move your enterprise forward. Networking is not an attempt to *cope* with reality. It *is* reality. Effective networking creates exactly the business environment best suited to *you*. It creates the world *you* need to do good business.

The First Two Things Every Networker Needs

Before you can adequately and effectively shape the reality you need, you need to ensure that you have what it takes to be an effective networker. It takes two things—at least to begin with—and the best way *I* know to tell you about them is to talk about the person I know best: *me*.

I have kept every condolence note and card I received after the deaths of my mother and father. I must have more than two hundred of them. From time to time, I look at them. Doing so brings back the pain of loss, but also the joy of their presence. Most of all, it reminds me that two people had love and concern for me, and this, in turn, reminds me of just what it is that holds the world together: the love and concern of one human being for another.

After my father died in 2002, I went to Columbus to meet with the Commercial Division Chief for the Board of Tax Assessors. As we started to talk, she said, "You're Dick Steele's son, aren't you? I'm sure sorry about your father's death. He was such a great man. He was always nice to everybody."

"That was my father. I miss him more than I can say."

"I know this is hard for you. I lost my mother last year."

In tears, we shared the pain of losing a parent. After we both had regained our composure, the assessor personally pulled all the files I needed. Usually, an assessor has time to do nothing more than point you in the right direction, and then you retrieve the files yourself. My new friend saved me a lot of time, and she made sure I had absolutely everything I needed.

As soon as I got back to Atlanta, I sat down and wrote her a card. "You are a special person," I wrote. "I came to get tax information, and I walked out blessed. Thank you for helping me today."

About two years later, I needed to consult the tax files again. I drove to Columbus and walked into her office. She was talking with two of her staff.

"Here's the nicest man in the entire world!" she smiled in my direction. "I want everybody in here to know that if Mr. Steele needs something, we'll help get it for him immediately."

Remarkable as this was, it was hardly the first time something like this had happened to me. Reach out to another person, and, chances are, you'll be met with an embrace. I hadn't sent the card to manipulate her. What I said in it was just how I felt. She had shown me compassion, and I thanked her. Because that thanks was given from no ulterior motive and without expectation of anything in return, it was received as a gift—a gift whose value was out of all proportion to the very little effort it cost me. My thanks made her feel good, feel good about our contact, about the way we had transacted our business, and even about herself. So, it also made her feel good about me, and it moved her to go the extra mile for me the next time we met. I didn't *try* to make this happen, but what I did made it happen, nevertheless.

Empathy has a powerful magic. We come to expect empathy from our family and close friends—but from *clients*? Well, I've never withheld my empathy from anyone, and I can tell you that when a business associate has extended to me a hand in understanding and love, it may be even more powerful than the same from a family member.

We lost our son, James Andrew Steele, on October 10, 2017. Roughly sixteen or seventeen years earlier, he was diagnosed with bipolar disease and extreme anxiety. I could write two or three books about Andrew without exhausting the examples of what a wonderful person he was, how kind and generous he was to everyone, the many things he did for others when he could barely do for himself. Still, I never gave up on his outliving me until I found him asleep forever in his bedroom that late October afternoon. I won't, I can't go into what we learned from many different psychologists and psychiatrists over the years. Suffice it to say that Andrew lived much longer than they anticipated. But it was hardly long enough.

After Andrew died, the world became a lot less fun place for me and my family. Our family continues to struggle with his not being with us. In the immediate aftermath, I withdrew from most of my activities. In all honesty, I often went to bed praying to God that I would not wake up the following morning. Death is sad for those left behind, but the death of a child, in my experience, has got to be the toughest of them all. At this time, I finished closing Steele Technology Partners because it was not doing well financially, and, even more, because I did not want to deal with it any longer. I did not leave our home very often, other than to pick up groceries, go to a doctor's appointment, visit a grief counselor, or be with one or both of our other two children and our grandchildren. Then, in late February 2018, I received an email from a dear friend, wonderful human being, senior technology executive, and a client of mine across three companies, Elizabeth Hoemeke. In 2018, she was a senior technology executive at Elavon, and today she is the CIO of One Inc. She wrote in her email that she looked forward to seeing me in our regular booth at McKendrick's Steak House on Friday at 11:30 a.m. I responded that I must have missed an earlier email because I did not have anything on my calendar about meeting that week or any week with her.

She replied: *I did not ask you about your calendar, I told you that I looked forward to seeing you Friday at 11:30 am at McKendrick's.*

At that moment, it seemed like the most loving thing anyone has ever said to me. People who love you enough not to take no for an answer when reaching out to comfort you are the most valuable friends you can have.

Still, I had mixed emotions. I had not been out in public to any degree with anyone but family and maybe a few very long-time, very close friends. I just wasn't sure that I was ready. But I did not want to offend her. So, I got dressed that morning and drove to McKendrick's Steak House. Elizabeth and I hugged, and we sat at Table 93, where we had sat many, many times over the years. When the waiter arrived, Elizabeth ordered a nice bottle of red. In all our prior twenty-five or thirty lunches over a dozen years, we had never ordered wine at lunch.

We exchanged pleasantries, but very quickly Elizabeth asked how I was doing. The question was the beginning of nearly an hour of tears running down my cheeks. In front of God and a nearly packed steak house, I wept as Elizabeth held my hand and shared an emotional time with me. I was not ashamed of my tears, but I felt horrible about putting Elizabeth through what most people would find a very uncomfortable, maybe agonizing, situation.

But when I could look up at her, it was obvious that she did not care what anyone in the restaurant was seeing or thinking. She was in the moment being there for me. *That* is the very heart of empathy, and as I write these words, the tears flow again—but now, in part at least, they flow from the recollection of the beauty of that moment in my life. I will never forget that moment. It was truly cathartic, starting me back on the road to something like normal.

Since that meal with Elizabeth, I have been "tested" a number of times on whether I really did learn deep lessons on empathy, and it has happened in a number of ways. We were blessed to have three amazing children. Each one was unique, and they were all loved by their teachers, their friends, their parent's friends and more than life itself, loved deeply by their parents and they still are.

When Andrew, turned fifteen or so, he began showing signs of problems. He was diagnosed with "Bi-Polar Level Two with extreme anxiety." I could go on and on sharing some very powerful stories and some very painful times. Why do I share any of Andrew's story in a book about networking? First, the lesson about empathy made me a better and much more empathetic human being and it is an emotion each of us need to be more receptive to give and receive. Second, Andrew's death and my willingness to be open and vulnerable about the experience has been helpful to others.

Within a few days of Andrew's passing, I wrote a very long Facebook post about his amazing life, his impact on others, and how his death had changed our world. I cried buckets of tears as my fingers hit the keys. It was the hardest thing I have ever written. A lot of folks would choose not to be that open and vulnerable to others, outside of their immediate family and friend's. My immediate family would fall into that camp. I did not want to share the experience. I needed to share the experience, because mental illness is running rampant in our country and far too many people, especially young people are dying as a result. Issues brought out into the open have a way of getting addressed much quicker than issues we only talk about behind closed doors. It is okay to not feel okay, regardless of a whether your pain is a temporary issue in your life or if you have been diagnosed with a more complex mental health issue. My goal was to stimulate conversation which did happen in a number of ways and continues to happen to me as late as a lunch I had on, July 10, 2022.

As you might imagine, the post received hundreds of responses from "Care," "Love" and empathetic messages galore. Many of those messages have been read by me dozens of times. I am writing this final section of the book in August of 2022, the month Andrew was born and just two months shy of the fifth anniversary of Andrew's death. Since my original Facebook post, I have written about Andrew often, posted many happy photos and shared some of his joys and his hardships. I never miss sharing something on his birthday and on each October 10, the day he left this world and the tremendous mental anguish he suffered through for the last sixteen or seventeen years of his life.

If you have read either the first or second edition of this book, you will notice that I quote far fewer statistics or cite particular networking technologies than I did in my first two books. Instead, I've added more stories that come from experiences and feelings deep within my heart. Great history and truth have been shared through stories over the thousands of years. I hope that my personal and often painful stories will motivate, inspire and encourage you to perhaps "borrow" an idea or an action that I found helpful to use it as your own, tweak it to what better represents who you are, but please do not just write them off if you truly want to have a life filled with deep meaning and deeper friendships.

As you can imagine, sharing the stories about the death of Andrew was and still is often very painful, but relating them is also healing to my soul. In this crazy world we live in now and after Covid-19 and the craziness of the far-right wing political activities, sane people are looking for people who have the guts to expose their deepest pain in hopes that it can help others. Most humans are looking for honesty, transparency and folks with an open heart and no agenda other than to help others.

In June of 2019, four months shy of the second anniversary of Andrew's death, I received a call or maybe it was an email from the executive assistant of a very well-known and highly successful CEO of a Fortune 500 company asking me to lunch. My immediate thought was I had won the lottery and that my recent re-entering the staffing industry as a sales executive, after I had taken almost two years off, was about to relaunch, and I was going to once again make the Big Money I had not made since 2015.

We met at the appointed time and had a great conversation about life, business, a not for profit we were both involved with at that time, and probably some football talk. I don't remember exactly how the conversation suddenly shifted, but what followed affected me in a deep and moving way. Today, I am still engaged in the deeper conversation with this same executive. This person said to me something to the effect of: "You probably wonder why I asked to have lunch." It was hard for me not to respond with "Because God has answered my prayers and my career is going to once again go into hyper-drive." But I did not.

His next words were about my sharing the struggle, the pain, the angst and all of the other emotions I experienced and shared over the previous two years on social media. He then said that he was facing a similar situation with one of his children and asked if I would be willing to answer a few questions. I was floored. First, this man is iconic, and I know very few people who have accomplished as much as he has or have been recognized for their success as often. On the surface, most people would swap lives with him in a heartbeat without reservation. However, looks are often deceiving and what I learned going through what we went through with Andrew for seventeen years is that mental illness does not respect your family name, your W-2, your 401K, your country club membership, or your attendance in a family of faith. Mental illness is running rampant in our country, killing far too many of our young folks every single day. Sadly, far too many "professionals" who call themselves psychiatrists and psychologists are as lost as a ball in high weeds. They are making a great living, yet it sure seems to me that their patients mean no more to them than any other product that other "professionals" sell or service. How or why would the Senior Psychiatrist at one of the most reputable hospitals in the country fire a patient who attempts suicide? Ponder that one for a minute because I have been pondering it for more than seven years.

Since the lunch my friend and I shared in June of 2019, I began praying for this young man daily, checking with his dad fairly often and discreetly chatting when we see each other at events around the city. I am more than humbled that this man was willing to share his situation with me, he trusted me enough to ask for help and to have further conversations about his son over the last three years.

Was this a one-off atypical experience? No.

Since that lunch, there have been numerous meetings with other friends, from the CIO of a major fin/tech company to CEOs of startup companies, as well as a few other folks in my life who have either lost a child to mental illness or they have a child in the middle of a mental health crisis.

Am I an expert on anything to do with mental health issues? Of course not. However, I have street smarts, and my wife and I experienced some seventeen tough years doing the best that we could. We fought just as hard as Andrew did to find a cure, a medicine, a program, or anything to help him enjoy this world. Personally, I failed often at empathy, but by watching my amazing, loving, forgiving wife on a day-to-day basis, I am much more of an empathic person than I could have ever imagined being twenty years ago.

If you are willing to be transparent with others and share your pain and your victories, you will attract those who are in pain and need help. It is often no more than a kind word, offer of prayer or a funny story about something that happened along the way as well as how to best survive the difficult times dealing with a mental health system that is horribly broken in our country to make a difference in another life. Be real. From time to time, it will hurt like hell, but the joy of hearing victories that others are experiencing, that you never experienced in your own situation, is amazingly cathartic.

This is Transparency 101, and if you are willing to live a transparent life, you will experience the true heart of relationships and although you may or may not do business with any of the folks you meet through difficulties, you will be compensated richly through the experience.

What unique experiences have you been through that by sharing openly, might open a conversation with a family member, neighbor, friend, or colleague? Begin by sharing just that.

We all have extraordinary events that we have experienced that have made us who we are. Some of those turned out well and you have a story of victory to encourage others. Some experiences were tragic, but the pain that we experienced has given others a window into what they are facing and what options they may have and finally, it can give offer hope, regardless of what they still face.

In the Book of Galatians, we are taught to "Bear One Another's Burdens." Volunteer to be a shock absorber, helping to soften the pain of life that from time to time is filled with bumps, rocky roads, and unsettling terrain. If you are there during the difficult times, you will have a relationship that includes being the first person invited to experience the joy and beauty of the times that are filled with mountain top experiences, happiness and victory. Furthermore, you will have someone willing to be your shock absorber when the road turns treacherous at some point, as it does for each and every one of us during our time on this earth.

Here, then, is item number one in your networking inventory: *The willingness to make contact with your own giving goodness as a human being.*

We all are going to leave this planet one day. My tombstone will read:

Richard E. Steele, Jr
1952—20__

What is important is not the date of my birth or the date of my death. The important part is the dash in the middle. Did I live a life worthy of God's calling? Did I live a life of service to my wife, children, family, and friends? If I did not, my life was in vain. That would be tragic for me, but it would also be tragic for you, too. Each of us has a measure of goodness inside, and if we are not willing to dig it out, others will never have the opportunity to be blessed by it.

Giving without Expecting

With the willingness to make contact with your own giving goodness comes item number two: *The desire to give without expecting anything in return.*

When I was a neophyte networker, I'd call someone I'd done something for or helped in some way, and I'd drawl, "Hey, friend! I need a favor. Could you help me do this?"

Sometimes the answer was "Sure! What do you need?" But sometimes that exclamation point was missing from the voice on the other end of the phone, and sometimes the word *sure* wasn't spoken. And then, sometimes, the response was, "Well, I'm real busy. In fact, my deadline for this project was last week, and I really don't have time to get with you."

Now, when that was the response I got, I wasn't always willing just to say goodbye, hang up the phone, and dial somebody else. Sometimes, I was ticked.

"Look," I might say, "I recently sent you two pieces of business. One was worth $5,000, and the second was worth $10,000. That does not include the Elton John tickets, front row center, for your wife, if I remember correctly. I'm asking you to do something for me that will probably take you less than an hour. Give me a break, *please!*"

This approach has actually worked for me—if you consider a successful outcome shaming someone into giving you help. The fact was that even if I got the favor I solicited, I was embarrassed when it was over, and I had either severely damaged a friendship or killed it dead. Emotional extortion, an appeal to the one-hand-washes-the-other quid-pro-quo ethic, may get you what you want—*once*—but it is no way to build, maintain, reinforce, or expand a network. Any transaction that leaves one or both parties feeling bad is a dead end, at best a short-term gain that sacrifices a long-term relationship.

Even the very best networkers fall far short of sainthood. If someone grabs each and every time you offer but is unwilling to give in return when he has the opportunity to do so, don't get self-righteous, don't get angry, and don't try to shame him into coming through for you. But do understand that you don't have to keep on giving to him. Your thought might be, "I'm not sure I want to do business with this person. He's not honorable. He has no ethics." I've walked away from a lot of people like that. Neither networks nor business can be sustained by one-way relationships. But recognizing this truth does not give me license to go around thinking people owe me something just because I've served them in some way. Give freely, without expecting anything in return, but avoid doing business with those who do nothing other than take and take and take.

Willing To Go "All In"

I don't remember the first funeral I ever attended but I assume it was a cousin or sibling of my grandparents in Senoia, Newnan, or Fayetteville, Georgia. I do remember before many of these early funerals, the body was sitting in a coffin in the middle of the living room of their home open for the guests to see. It felt strange that most of the men were standing in the room smoking cigarettes, eating off paper plates and perhaps drinking adult beverages in a plastic cup while Aunt Estelle or Uncle Homer were laying there a few feet away.

The first funeral I remember in great detail was for a young lady I grew up with beginning in kindergarten, who was murdered on her job during college. It was my first time as a pallbearer and her death at twenty-two years of age in 1974, still lives in me forty-eight years later. What I remember most is how much it meant to her mom, dad, brother, and sister to have so many loving friends at their home for the entire time the police were investigating the case and at their home after the funeral. Although I probably did not know what the word "empathy" meant at that time, I experienced it in a powerful way, and it has stuck with me ever since that day.

I have never forgotten that lesson and for that reason, I attend many more funerals than most folks who do not work in the funeral industry. I am often asked why I attend so many funerals and my always-looking-for-a-punchline mentality replies: "I am afraid if I don't go to their funeral, they won't come to mine." There are several funny stories that resulted from folks not understanding that quip was my attempt at humor that I would love to share, but not now.

Today, every morning, I read the *Columbus, Georgia Ledger Enquirer* newspaper to see if I have lost a friend from high school or one of their parents. Seventy-five percent of the trips I make to Columbus these days are for funerals. I also watch Facebook to see if a loved one of a friend has passed so that I know whether to either attend a funeral or send a condolence card. Having seen empathy for Ann's family in action back in 1974, I believe our showing love to those in our lives when they are most vulnerable is not a choice, it is a responsibility as a human being.

Over the last 48 years, I have seen the results time after time. I will share just one out of what could be a long list of individual experiences. The funerals in Atlanta and Columbus include people that I knew and some that I did not. Traveling to Augusta, Chattanooga, Nashville, Defuniak Springs, Florida and many other cities were, for the most part, to honor and celebrate folks that I have never met, but I have a relationship with one or more of their family members.

If you sincerely care about your family, friends, colleagues, clients and prospects, you have a choice to make. Are you going to be there for them when it is convenient for you or are you willing to commit the same wager that poker players make when their chips are down, and they face elimination? They declare that they are "All In." Should we not be "All In" for those whom we love, depend on, or earn a living through serving? I definitely say we should, and I do my best to practice being "All in" as often as possible.

I would love to share some very personal, yet inspiring moments from funerals I attended over the years when I was not on the "expected guest" list. But for the sake of brevity, I will share just one, because it means so much to me.

A few years ago, I saw a Facebook post that the mom/mother in-law of two folks I love and enjoy spending time with whenever possible, had died. Dave and Monika Hudson are dear friends. They are also powerful and respected folks in our Atlanta technology community.

Both had reached out to me when we lost Andrew in 2017, and out of their extreme kindness, they took Beth and me out to dinner after we closed Steele Technology Partners. It was the best meal that we could not have afforded to do by ourselves that year, due to the fact that we lost most of our life's savings when we closed Steele Technology Partners.

Although they knew we would survive, their gift of dinner and an amazing bottle of wine was because they were sharing their love and empathy. When I read the news of Dave's mom passing, there was no question as to what I was going to do. The funeral was a few days later 280+ miles from Atlanta in Defuniak, Florida. I cleared my schedule for that day and left early for the 4.5-hour drive. I was standing outside of the church, about to walk in, when the family was moving from the family room to the entrance to be seated for the service. At some point, my eyes locked with Monika's, and we both immediately had tears welling up in our eyes. Although, we had not talked at all during the days before the service, she looked at me and said: "I knew you would be here." Tears moved from gathering in our eyes to flowing, without reservation or regret. I then hugged Dave and got out of the way so they could join the processional going inside. After the services, everyone was invited to dinner in the community hall and the food was divine, much like what was served fifty years earlier at the family small town funerals. Baked ham, turkey, chicken, at least ten different vegetables prepared in as many ways as possible to prepare them and a long table of desserts that I almost pulled my chair up to so I could sample every one, rather than going back and forth.

Over the next hour, we shared the beauty of true communion with a lot of people I had never met and probably will not ever see again in this lifetime. It was an experience of how I imagine banquets will be in Heaven. I did not need my car to make the return drive back to Atlanta. I floated on the peace that came from a loss that through the power of love and empathy became magical.

Why are these funeral stories in a book on networking? It is a story about the value of true relationships, which *are* the heart of networking.

It is truly about making the decision to go "all in" with the people in your life. True, some of the funerals have been for a family member of a past or current client, but long before they were clients, they were friends. As I've said, I don't have any clients. I do business with friends and friends of friends. Some of the funerals have been for relatives of friends that I have begged for business from over the years, but they had another partner doing a great job or it was not within their power to use my service. That fact did not change or alter our relationship.

Since the beginning of time, but even more so after this past 2.5 years of Covid-19 woes, people are looking for people who are real. People who want to give for no other reason than because it is always the right thing to do. My intent in this edition of *The Heart of Networking* is to be as real as I can possibly be, showing you my heart as best as I can do that.

A Salesman's Heresy

I've been in a number of different businesses, but always a big part of each of them has been increasing the company's revenue. I make a lot of sales, but I've never had to sell anybody anything. If you've read a book or two on "salesmanship" or attended the odd sales seminar now and then, you've almost certainly run across the "ABC" formula. It stands for "Always Be Closing," and it's the attitude every successful salesman is "supposed" to have. Everything he says, everything he does is supposed to be directed toward closing the sale. The idea is to narrow your relationships down to the diameter of a pinprick, so that each relationship has but a single purpose: to close a sale.

I've never believed in the ABC formula. For me, it's a straitjacket. Am I interested in making a sale? Of course! Although my children are all grown and financially on their own, I still have bills to pay, food to buy, and at my age, medical expenses occur much more often than they did earlier in life. But what I'm *more* interested in is having a relationship with somebody, because this transforms the sales process. There's no secret system at work here. It's as simple as this: Given the opportunity, people buy from people they like. True, sometimes they'll buy exclusively on price, and when they do, I'm usually not going to be their go-to guy. Whatever I've sold, my primary product has always been service, service, and more service. Even if you're not greedy for mile-wide profit margins, it's impossible to give champagne service at draft-beer prices. But if a potential customer is shopping for value, not just price, chances are he or she will buy from me, because I offer the greatest value of all: a relationship.

Offering the value of a relationship is not always easy or even obvious. The way I look at it, I'm out there to serve. When I go into a room, I'm looking to make friends and form relationships with people who may or may not blossom into clients someday. I want to meet people I don't know, and I want to visit with people I do know, so that I can be more receptive to the needs they have in their lives. If someone has a need that I can fulfill by selling him something, fantastic! But—and here's the part that's neither easy nor obvious—if he has a need, I can fulfill by introducing him to someone else, that's just fine, too.

When I help set up a business transaction from which I will not profit immediately or directly, when I've introduced people to each other and money changes hands without even passing through mine, what do I get out of it? In the short term, I get the joy of knowing I have helped two people solve a common problem. And if that turns out to be all I get, well, it's a great enough feeling that it counts for a whole lot. But, over the longer term, at some point in the future, one or both of those people may need something that I *can* offer, and, when this happens, they'll be inclined to buy it from *me*. Or even if neither one of them is in the market, they may steer some other customer to me. My sense is that about at least 15 percent of my business comes from people whose business I initially sent elsewhere because, at the time, that's where it belonged.

I have been very fortunate over my career to sell between $50 million and a $100 million dollars in products and services over the last fifty-plus years. I want to win every single pitch that I make, but I have never prayed to win a piece of business regardless of how much my company may need it just to survive. I do my best to have a short time of prayer and reflection before going into any sales meeting or meeting with a potential new hire. This clears the clutter and focuses me on the task at hand. I try to find a quiet place, be it my car in the parking lot, the restroom, or the lobby. I ask God to give me "favor" in the eyes of the person or team I am about to meet. It is something that God gave to Ruth, the young Moabite woman who was married to an Israeli man who died. Ruth was given favor in the eyes of Boaz, and in my faith practice, it changed the rest of history. Praying to win against another person or company is selfish. Praying for favor, however, opens the door for a deep relationship that is worth more over the long run than any single piece of business today.

Being granted favor over the last fifty years has provided a significant income to our family over many years. With income that size, I should be sitting well in my semi-retirement. However, all that glitters is not gold, and when you gamble as an entrepreneur, you have some companies that do not go as well as you planned. As a result, I have also experienced at least four or five years of $0.00 income over my career. The zero income years were because I sold a business and took time off, I was fired or quit a job and it took over a year to find new work, or during two start-up companies where I worked without a salary while investing our savings into the company. What the late great Jim McKay, first said on TV's *Wide World of Sports* when it debuted in 1961, I have personally experienced on numerous occasions: "The thrill of victory and the agony of defeat." It has often been from the agony of defeat that I have learned some of the greatest lessons. It is not always what I did right or wrong, but how I handled the experience. Sometimes, it was a revelation as to who were true friends and who only cared for me only when I was the one buying drinks. These are the lessons that change the future.

As an owner and usually the lead salesperson or as a sales executive for other companies, I am very aware that growing revenue is why we are in business and staying in business. Nothing really happens in a business until someone buys your goods or services. One principle that has stuck with me over the years is to celebrate the victories in an over-the-top way because they need to be celebrated. Conversely, you should never beat yourself to death over a defeat. You can very rarely find an undefeated sports team. Everyone has good and bad days, but if you refuse to quit, you always have an opportunity to reverse the loss and perhaps score a much larger deal around the corner.

Taking Inventory So Far

From the get-go, being an effective networker requires two vital items in your personal inventory: *The willingness to make contact with your own giving goodness as a human being* and *The desire to give without expecting anything in return.* I still have some more to say about this second item, and I'll say it in a moment or two; however, first, I want to cover four more inventory items essential to the attitude of the effective networker:

Availability
The willingness to listen and to give
Character and integrity
Charisma

Availability. Networkers are available. Too many people go through life so fast and furiously that when they're with people, they're not really with them at all. Their bodies are right there in the room, but their attention is elsewhere, usually projected into the immediate future, thinking about the next meeting—which, when they physically attend that, will be as wasted as the present meeting, because they'll be thinking about the meeting that comes after that. And so it goes with so many people. Their mental presence is out of sync with their physical presence. They're here, but they're absent.

If you're going to be effective as a networker, you have to be fully present, physically, mentally, emotionally, all of the time. You have to be authentic. Businesspeople who schmooze at a cocktail party are not effective networkers. Trivial party small talk, banter, posturing, these things can be highly entertaining, but they aren't manifestations of genuine availability.

The willingness to listen and to give. All effective networkers are good listeners and good givers. They are willing to listen not until *they* are tired of listening, but until the other person gets tired of talking. In response, they offer themselves as fonts of helpful information. The effective networker presents himself as an answer to the other person's need. He may not be able to solve all the problems to which he listens, but he makes it his business to share ownership of those problems and provide as much helpful information as possible.

Character and integrity. Genuine networkers don't try to create an artificial vortex that sucks others into their circle of influence. They portray themselves accurately, without inflating their level of authority, influence, or potential. Many people spend their lives using their "power" to impress people. If you want to be truly charismatic, your life will be characterized not by how many people you've impressed but how many you've served.

Charisma. Networkers are charismatic—in a genuine, positive way. If you sense that someone is networking based on such superficial attractions as power, energy, looks, or gender, run in the other direction. True charisma, the force that consistently attracts others to you, is based on integrity and dignity combined with power. This kind of charisma endures. It has the staying power to help create the broadest, most effective networks.

Help Wanted: Servant

So now we have a total of six items you need to have ready in your personal inventory before you embark on the networking enterprise. Let's go back to item number two: *The desire to give without expecting anything in return.* If you want to know exactly what this means, let me put it this way. You see the following employment ad— *Help Wanted: Servant.* And you jump at it. *That's* the desire to give without expecting anything in return. When I was a teenager in Columbus, back in the mid-1960s, during the war in Vietnam, I read about a rally being held in Atlanta at the Fulton County Stadium. The keynote speaker was Secretary of State Dean Rusk, and the entertainment was Anita Bryant and Kate Smith. (If this does not date this story by well over a half-century, nothing else I could share would.)

Like just about everyone else back then, I was troubled and confused about Vietnam, and I thought that attending the rally might clarify things for me. I heard there was going to be a motor coach from Columbus to Atlanta for the event, and I asked my dad if I could go and if he would help me with a ticket. He agreed, and, the morning of the rally, dropped me off at the back of the local high school, where the bus was waiting.

I was just about the only person my age interested in that rally. Fortunately, I knew a few of the adults on the bus, but I did feel a little uncomfortable. All the way to Atlanta, I sat in the back of the bus, next to an ice chest filled with soft drinks and a big bag of snacks. People came to the back to get a drink or a pack of crackers. Since I was sitting right by the cooler, I began opening it and serving the drinks. Then it occurred to me that others might want a drink but did not feel comfortable trying to walk down the aisle of a swaying bus. I don't know why, really, but I soon found myself walking up the aisle and taking orders. I did this for the rest of the ride to Atlanta and on the return trip home.

It was an inspiring show. You only had to hear Kate Smith sing "God Bless America" once in your life to remember it forever. I had a great time on the trip and never felt like I was working. When we arrived back in Columbus, my dad was waiting for me. Most of the passengers on the bus came over to dad and told him that I had made the trip more enjoyable for everyone. The leader of the excursion gave me the money my dad had paid for my ticket. He said that everyone on the bus voted to split the cost of my fare.

Dad was proud, and, at that point in my life, I don't suppose I had given him much to be proud of on a regular basis. I felt a warmth of satisfaction I had never felt before. I had discovered my passion: to serve.

These days you often read about "servant leadership." There are even colleges and business schools that include servant leadership as part of their curriculum. One of my heroes and mentors for forty-some of my first seventy years on this earth was the late Mr. William B. Turner, retired chairman of the Executive Committee for both the W. C. Bradley Group and Synovus Financial Corporation, both based in Columbus, and a former member of The Coca-Cola Company Board of Directors where his grandfather was the first Chairman of the Board. Mr. Turner wrote a book called *The Learning of Love: A Journey Toward Servant Leadership*. It is the most meaningful treatment of the subject I have ever read. Another Columbus business icon, Mr. Jimmy Blanchard, today chairman emeritus of the board of Synovus, has taken Mr. Turner's lessons to the next level. Every year since 1998, *Fortune Magazine* has named Synovus one of the top twenty companies to work for in America. In 1999, Synovus was honored by *Fortune* as *the* number one company to work for in America. I think anyone in Synovus or anyone who has watched from the outside would agree that one of the primary reasons for this success is the servant leadership example of Mr. Blanchard. If you ever have the pleasure of hearing Mr. Turner, Mr. Blanchard, or any other key executive from the Synovus family speak, you will learn more about people, love, giving, and being accountable than you will learn about deposits and loans.

Another great example of servant leadership was the late Mr. Truett Cathy, chairman of Chick-fil-A. He not only created one of the fastest-growing, most successful fast-food empires, he also built orphanages in north Georgia, sponsored summer camps for some 1,600 children, and financed scholarships for more than 16,500 college students. The bulk of his time was devoted to meeting the needs of others. Perhaps the most dramatic example of this is his decision to keep all Chick-fil-A stores closed on Sunday. Please name another major national fast-food chain that is closed on Sunday. You cannot. For this one important day each week, Mr. Cathy did not hesitate to honor his Creator and to put people before profits. Even if he had done nothing else, giving his employees time with their families would earn Truett Cathy a prominent niche in the Servant Hall of Fame, if there were such a place.

Dr. Martin Luther King, Jr. summed it all up beautifully in one of his speeches. "Everybody," he said, "can be great, because anybody can serve. You don't have to have a college degree to serve. You don't have to make your subject and your verb agree to serve. You don't have to know about Plato and Aristotle to serve. You don't have to know Einstein's theory of relativity to serve. You don't have to know the second theory of thermodynamics to serve. You only need a heart full of grace. A soul generated by love."

Mr. Blanchard and Mr. Cathy are fine examples, and I am sure you know of others. But the question for you and me is *Am I an example?*

If not, why not?

If not, why not begin today?

I find that when my motivation is to serve, I always win. When my goal is focused not on making a sale but on helping my prospect succeed, I know I will not be forgotten. What is the benefit of making an introduction that results in giving someone else business? Satisfaction and the joy of knowing I helped two people solve a common problem, added to the likelihood that I've created potential business, a customer for the future. I don't need to make all my money right this minute.

Our job in life is very simple. You and I are on this planet to serve others. Despite the idea you get walking through the mall or watching TV, one commercial after another, people don't really want to buy merchandise. They want even less to buy something just because *you* need to sell it to them. I know for a fact that nobody gets up in the morning and says, "I wonder what Steele is selling today? I like him a lot, and I'd like to buy twelve of whatever he's selling, just because he has a wife and financial needs."

Nobody wants to be sold anything. People want to buy and they want to buy from people they like and people they trust.

So instead of entering a conversation like a salesman, thinking *What merchandise can I sell this guy today?* I come into the talk with a servant mentality, thinking, *What may I offer today to solve this person's problems?* Not only does this approach allow me to help someone, which gives me joy, it also identifies me as a servant.

For me, "servant" does not connote a slave to be exploited or a doormat to be walked on, but a person who is always available: the go-to guy. In the short run, I may end up giving somebody else business. For the long run, however, I have sold myself to two individuals as the go-to guy. As I mentioned earlier, I believe that about 15 percent of the people I introduce to one another do eventually direct business to me. If our lives were snapshots, success or failure would depend solely on the sale you make or fail to make right now. But our lives are much more like movies, which means that the sale you *don't* make in scene 1 may well set up sales in scenes 6, 10, and 35. If you stop at scene 1, you come out a failure. If you let the movie keep playing, who knows? If I want to be a successful networker, I can't cut someone out of my life just because he does not or cannot give me some business at the moment I ask for it. As the movie rolls on, one day, she may become chairman of the board of a company I want to do business with. One day, she may pass my name along to someone who does need what I'm selling.

That brings me to another article of attitude necessary in the networker's personality portfolio: *patience.*

Never bring a snapshot mentality to the movie that is life. Done right, networking offers the ongoing satisfaction of serving others. Instant gratification, however, is another matter. You usually won't get it. Networking is about creating a reality around you, one that, over time, makes your business more possible to do more profitably. Genesis says it took God six days to make the world. You and I are not the Almighty (regardless of what we think we see in the mirror), so it may take us years to put together even our little corner of world. But it's time well invested, no matter how long it takes.

One of the realities even the most dedicated servant must face is that you can't serve everyone. Your time is limited. Often, you'll have to make decisions about whom to meet and whom to pass up. Don't leave these important decisions to the spur of the moment. Set out your priorities. For me, it is my faith, then my family. Unless my family has an immediate need of me, my priority is to my boss and the company. Next come my non-profit or community responsibilities. After that, it's everybody else.

The Place of Passion . . .

Maybe I'm being a little too flip in talking about the attributes of a good networker as so many "inventory items." Certainly, I have a hard time thinking about the next indispensable element as an item in some inventory, but we have to talk about it—precisely because it *is* indispensable.

Some folks say that great salespeople are born, not made. True, these people admit, you can train yourself to be a pretty good salesperson. You can learn the seven steps of selling. You can take a networking course. You can have a fundamental business background or an Ivy League MBA. And you can do okay. But what you cannot learn is passion. No university or business school offers Passion 101. It's either inside of you, or it isn't, and, as some people see it, that means either you're born with it or you're not.

In my experience, I have seen individuals I would indeed call born salespeople. Untutored, unsophisticated, they could nevertheless sell anything. But my experience also suggests to me that we're *all* born salespeople. If you're making even a barebones living, you are a salesperson. You've managed to sell at least one person on the idea of paying you to do something. The real difference between those we generally call born salespeople and everyone else is that the *born* salespeople are in touch with their passion and can connect that passion to whatever they're selling. Can you learn passion? No. Can you learn to make contact with the passion we're all born with? Absolutely. It's what they call finding the fire in your belly.If you find it impossible to connect your passion with whatever it is you're selling, start looking for something else to sell. If you cannot connect your passion with the idea of serving others, don't try to become a networker. Find your passion, connect it with something to do, and then get busy doing it.

Now, some people complain that they are passionate, but also shy or introverted; therefore, despite their passion, they can't sell, and they can't network.

If you are an introvert, you need to realize one thing. You are unique; nobody else is exactly like you. You have a wealth of qualities to share, which no one else can offer. That means they're precious, and that means that people want to know all about them. Start by connecting with something you are most passionate about. Follow that passion, and let it direct you to an environment in which you are most comfortable. In other words, start networking with people who share some of your interests. There are "MeetUp" groups in every city in this country that are focused on every subject from "Ruby on Rails" to bird watching, climbing mountains or playing poker. Visit "MeetUps," and you will be amazed at just how many people that would be fun to meet share something that is already part of your story. Once you find a level of comfort in such a group, you can begin your network there, and, via the network, you'll soon find your circle expanding to the outside. You may still feel shy. When you look in the mirror, you may still see an introvert—but now it will be an introvert who happens to have a lot of friends!

There's no such thing as a one-minute networking course, but then there are very few things in life that you can do well the first time you try. You fell several times before learning to ride a bicycle. You didn't run a marathon the first time you laced up your running shoes. If you start training as a networker now, you'll be pleasantly surprised by what you'll accomplish within a year.

. . . And Passion in its Place

A networker needs passion like an automobile needs fuel. However, a supertanker full of gasoline will get you nowhere unless it's run through an ignition system hooked to an engine hooked to a drive train hooked to wheels and all put together just right. The desire to network is absolutely necessary to networking, but it's not enough. You also need to organize yourself so that all this passion can be put to productive work.

The networker's final inventory item? *Organization.*

Decide what your business is. Get up each and every morning and stick with what you've decided. The fancy word for this is *commitment.* If you decide that your job is selling widgets, you can't rely on winging it: "When I get into the office, I'll figure out what I'm going to do today." Fully committed on Monday, you need to know what you're going to do next Thursday. Get into the habit of making plans and drawing up forecasts. Instead of figuring out what you're going to do today, you should be in a position to declare: "My goal this *year* is to meet fifty people who buy widgets. I have a list with two hundred names of people who buy widgets. I am ready to meet two of them at this meeting tonight."

Take the necessary time to set goals and to prepare to achieve them. You can always spot people who are prepared. They show up on time, and when they start talking, it is clear that they speak from a position of knowledge, having primed themselves with the information that enables them to hit the market running from the moment their feet touch the bedroom floor in morning.

Think about the last time you dealt with a well-prepared colleague, client, or salesperson. What did you feel? I'll bet it was something like admiration and maybe even a little envy. Now think about the last time you struggled with a colleague, client, or salesperson who, unprepared, tried to wing it on broken wings. Maybe you felt sorry for him. Maybe you were angry at having your time wasted. Whatever you felt, I'll bet it was anything *but* admiration and envy.

Preparation doesn't just make your job easier; it is essential to creating an environment receptive to you and your networking efforts. People want to work with people they admire. They don't want to work with people for whom they feel pity or find irritating. I was fortunate in 1987 to hear the brilliant Dr. Michael Mescon speak on the topic of preparation. He said that "90% of success is showing up, on time, dressed to play." *That* is commitment to the next level. Dr. Mescon, with his equally brilliant son, Dr. Timothy Mescon, later wrote a book expanding on the speech: *Showing Up for Work and Other Keys to Business Success* (Peachtree Publishers).

I think I learned my first real lessons about the importance of preparation from watching and working for professional baseball teams. In 1964, at the ripe old age of twelve, I worked as bat boy for the

Columbus Yankees, the Double A farm team of the New York Yankees. I met some of the most interesting and amazing people any boy could dream of meeting. Our home games started at 7:35 p.m. I had to be at the ballpark by 4:30 p.m. every day. I did not understand why so early—until my first day on the job. The pitchers generally arrive first. Everyone else on the team, other than that night's starting pitcher, was dressed and on the field by 5:00, a full two and a half hours before the game begins. I watched them run wind sprints, shag fly balls and grounders, and take batting practice. Around 6:45, they took infield practice from the team manager. Most players then relaxed for a few minutes, changed their uniforms, and were ready to hit the field when the "Star Spangled Banner" was played at 7:30.

If these guys do this sort of preparation to play a game for two or three hours six months out of the year, what makes you and me so darn special? We cannot forgo paying the price, not if we are truly interested in becoming good networkers and star employees in our companies.

I set my career goals by first looking backward. "This past year was great. I met twenty two of the thirty people I really wanted to meet." Great, yes, but the fact is that I had set thirty as my goal, so I will now devote some time and effort to determining why I didn't meet my goal. If, after reflection, I determine the goal is still viable, I'll incorporate it into next year's plan, and I'll begin figuring out what I can do in that year to achieve the goal I narrowly missed this year.

It's important to work hard, but it's hardly enough. In and of itself, working hard doesn't make me accountable. Goals are the marks on a yardstick. Either I reach those marks or I don't. Quantifiable goals keep us accountable. The great American philosopher and New York Yankee Hall of Fame catcher Yogi Berra said it best: "You've got to be careful if you don't know where you are going. You might not get there."

Just how organized do you have to be? We'll get into the details in the next two chapters, but the short answer is that you have to be *very* organized. You need a system to record and compile data on your contacts and clients. Collecting the name, address, phone number, and e-mail is just the beginning. That gets you into the game. To be a serious player, you need to get as much detail as possible on every person in your database: title, report-to, spouse, children, college, graduate degree, sports interest, religious affiliation, personal interests, city where born—any information you can glean from multiple sources.

Here's what I do when I meet someone for the first time at an event. I come to the event with a set goal for a first meeting. It is to find out enough to fill three or four 3-by-5 index cards with information I can transfer to my computer database. This doesn't mean I play Twenty Questions. I don't want to subject my new contact to the third degree. Instead, I ensure that I'm sufficiently prepared and organized to get all the information I need in the course of normal conversation. And my hope is that while I'm filling three or four index cards on him, he's getting only enough for half a card on me. If he can write more, that means I've done too much of the talking!

I'll go into this more in Chapter 4, but I want to give you an idea here and now about just how organized you need to be. I find that productive so-called spontaneous conversation is kind of a rare commodity. It's not so unusual as to be the stuff of myth, like an appearance of the Loch Ness monster, but you certainly cannot *rely* on its happening. This does not make conversation any less vital to networking; therefore, to enhance the opportunities for *productive* talk, I prepare thoroughly for "spontaneous conversation." I need to start filling my index cards.

Fortunately for me, as far back as I can remember, I've been fascinated by all life's details and have been desirous of learning all I can about what's happening in the world. When I was in high school, I subscribed to *Newsweek, Time,* and *U.S. News & World Reports,* and I read them all, cover to cover, every single week. Today, every day, I try to read several newspapers, as well as all the relevant business journals. I spend my first hour at work reading about new developments on the Web, reading articles from national publications, and blog posts, and I listen to podcasts. Staying current with events in America and around the world about technology, business in general, current events, not for profit organizations, and even entertainment news helps me relate to a wide variety of people. I also make it my business to comb through articles for news about companies or individuals with whom I do business or that do business with my clients. I look for information that might help me relate to someone or that might be of use to someone I know or want to know better.

Targeted, focused reading like this is great preparation for "spontaneous conversation," especially when it arms you with a news item you know will interest a person you are about to meet with. However, I don't restrict myself to only those articles I think will interest others. Often, I read an article for the simple reason that *I* find it interesting. At the time, that's as far as it goes. I may not think what I just read will ever be of any particular use to me or anyone else. Then, two days or a week later, I'll be in a conversation and someone will say, "Did you see the article about . . . ?"

"Oh yes," I'll reply. "That was fascinating, wasn't it? Can you believe they were able to . . . ?" And another apparently "spontaneous conversation" will be off and running as a truly meaningful exchange. As Louis Pasteur remarked, "Chance favors the prepared mind."

Reading doesn't make me who I am, but it rounds out the quality of content I can bring to any conversation or meeting. Many times, I've earned a seat at the table based not on my intellect, but on what I know. Engaging a potential network contact with information of genuine interest to him is an infinitely more effective way to start a conversation than with a question like "Hot enough for you?" Reading and more reading will not only furnish your mind for productive conversation, but it will also help you find partners for those conversations. As you read the local papers and the journals relevant to your industry, you'll soon notice the same names popping up time and time again. Take note of these names. Make a list. They are the people you must get to know. Just how to go about meeting them is the subject of the next chapter.

3

■

Connecting

MANY NOVICE NETWORKERS SPEND A LOT OF TIME WORRYING about what they're going to say when they meet "someone important." They worry about making a good impression and striking up a relationship. True, these are important things, but they're entirely hypothetical until you connect with "someone important." And before you can connect, you must determine who the "important" people are. That done, you need to find a route to your chosen prospect. Once you've accomplished these two objectives, it's time to start the conversation.

The road from one point in this journey to the next is typically paved with a little good fortune and a whole lot of research.

The Work of Networking

If I told you that "networking is getting to know people" I wouldn't be wrong, exactly, but I would be misleading. Effective networking really begins *after* you've gotten to know the people you want to recruit into your network. In other words, before you can recruit someone into your network, you must get to know him or her.

This smells like a catch-22 if there ever was one. How can you get to know someone *before* you get to know him or her?

You roll up your sleeves and get to work. I never approach an individual or go into a meeting with anyone without first doing some research on that person. My goal? To know more about her than her momma does! Now, I don't always reach that goal, but I can get pretty close, and I can get there before we even meet.

First, I go to online social networking sites, including LinkedIn, Facebook and any other site I think will be useful (see Chapters 5, 6, and 7), enter his or her name—let's call him Bill Smith—and read everything I can. I also do a Google search on Bill's name. Depending upon what area Bill Smith works in, I might even use a paid service to get information, but if Bill has rich LinkedIn and Facebook pages, this usually isn't necessary. Now, if I'm researching someone I've wanted to meet for a long time, there is a high probability that I have already entered him into my database and started a file on him containing clippings from newspapers, journals—anything I've found that mentions him. In addition, I often google "Mr. and Mrs. Joe Prospect." Many times, that has led to a treasure trove of information on charities they support as a family, speaking engagements where they were on the podium and even social events that they attended—photos included. I don't consider this "stalking," because every piece of information I collect was created and put on the internet for anyone and everyone to see by the person I am researching.

Once I have amassed as much information as I can within a reasonable period, I review it all thoroughly. What I am looking for especially is whatever things we may have in common. Maybe we're both Methodists, UGA football fans, community volunteers, or Dylan devotees. Perhaps we are both friends of another community leader. I also look for anything my target individual has in common with other people I already know and know well. Say Bill Smith holds a Harvard MBA. Well, I know that my friend Sheila has her MBA from Harvard, so I call her to ask if she knows Bill Smith well enough to make an e-mail or phone introduction on my behalf.

I don't stop with collecting information on the person. I read everything I can find about Bill Smith's company. If I know anyone at his company—or anyone who can put me in touch with someone at his company—I make more phone calls. My objective is to identify three people I know who work for Bill Smith's company. I call each of them and say, "Your company is one of my targets. I'm setting up a meeting with the vice president, Bill Smith. What can you tell me about him? What are some of the problems you see facing the company?" (If I use any of this information when I finally talk with Bill Smith—and I usually use a lot of it—I am always careful to avoid breaching confidentiality. I don't reveal who I've talked with, but instead keep what I say purposely vague: "I've been doing some research," I'll say. "This is what I know, and this is how I think I can help you.")

I get my information from everywhere. When I read an article about a person in my database, I can always discover another item or two to input. For example, I might run across "Bill Smith, long-time Lutheran . . ." or "Bill Smith, long-time Rotary club member . . . ," and then I know Bill is a Lutheran and a Rotarian.

I don't rely exclusively on online social networking and other Internet or print information. When I arrive for my appointment with Bill, I make sure to get to his office a little early, and I talk to his secretary or executive assistant. These people, close to the boss, are potential gold mines of information.

"How long have you worked for Bill?" I'll ask.

"Twelve years."

"That's unbelievable! I don't believe he's been here twelve years."

"No, I was with him at Reynolds."

"Oh, you must know him very well, then. He must be a good guy"

"He's a great guy! He's a very dedicated father. He'd rather be outdoors than in an office—loves to go sailing and spends every Friday afternoon at the golf course."

This is all valuable information that allows me to shape my conversation. I make it a rule never to discount anyone, especially receptionists, secretaries, and assistants. We are all important as human beings, of course, but support staff are especially important to me as sources of information about the executive I want to pull into my network. I have profited greatly from getting to know people whose names are not engraved on any brass plaque in the executive suite.

In the 1980s and 1990s, whenever I would visit the Ritz Carlton here in Atlanta, three doormen, Abner, Jim, and Laurence, treated me like a first cousin.

"Ricky! How're you doing?"

Then the doormen notice the people I'm with, and all of a sudden they're saying, "Good afternoon, sir. We're glad to have you at the Ritz Carlton, sir."

More than once, a person I'm with will ask, "How do you know those guys?"

"I used to be in the transportation business, and I did a lot of work with these men. I took a few of them out to lunch over the years. They're great guys. Laurence is studying for his real estate license now, and he knows everybody in town. I've met a number of people through him."

There's no reason to walk past a receptionist, secretary, doorman, or concierge without pausing, smiling at him or her, and saying, "Good morning. How are you doing today?" They're paid to say "good morning," but you aren't, and the fact that you pause, make eye contact, flash a smile, and voice a greeting makes a big impression that, like everything else you do, has an impact on the environment in which you do business.

When you get to Bill Smith's office, look at his assistant and say, "Good morning. How are you doing today?" Ask her about the picture of her son on her desk. Listen to her response.

Now, how much time did this exchange consume? All of thirty seconds, perhaps, and yet it made this person, who works with Mr. Smith all day, every day, feel good. When you call again next week or next month and ask to speak to her boss, she'll remember you.

If I'm with someone else, it's not always polite or feasible to hold him up while I chat with a doorman or receptionist for even thirty seconds. But whenever I *can* do it, I do it, and it never goes unnoticed.

"What you did out there was very kind," Bill Smith might say to me when we sit down in his office. "Do you do that everywhere you go?"

"Yes, sir, I try to. I know Ms. Jones also works hard, and I always like to learn something new from hard workers.

Mr. Smith raises his eyebrows, and I think I know what's going through his mind: *This guy is a little different. I'll take a bit more time and get to know him.* Or something of the sort. What I do know for certain is that time spent on kindness is never misspent.

The information I get from online and print sources is important, as is what I can grab from half a minute's talk with a receptionist or executive assistant. But I don't stop my research even after I'm inside my contact's office. I *look* at Bill Smith's office, intent on taking a mental snapshot, which I can use during the initial meeting or go over in my mind later, as I add more information to my Bill Smith database file. Based on what I see on his desk and walls, I might discover that Bill went to Clemson and played football there. He has model ships all over his office, sailing craft only, not a motor-driven vessel in the bunch. The picture on his desk reveals a wife and three kids. All this information will go into my database, and each time I meet with Bill Smith, I hope to walk away with even more information.

Is this an awful lot of work to go through for the sake of a contact or a sale? Yes, of course it is. But, then, I'm not manipulating Bill Smith to sell him something. I'm trying to create a relationship that will last for many, many years. Whether he ever buys anything from me or not, this relationship will be one more positive element in the world where I do business.

Finding the Movers and the Shakers

With whom should you network? Whom should you meet? Sometimes you already have the answer, and sometimes the answer is obvious. You have a widget to sell, and you know that Ms. Jones buys all the widgets for ABC Company. A meeting with her, therefore, is pretty much mandatory. It's easy to formulate a rule of thumb: Identify the people who have the power and authority to do business with you, target them for a meeting, and begin to create relationships with them.

If you don't know who the people with the requisite power and authority are, find out. Do your homework. Read the local papers, industry directories, and industry journals. I used to recommend the reference departments of the larger public libraries but today is not 2005 when the first edition of this book was published. Today is 2022, and I don't believe you can find in any library anything current that is not even more current on the internet. And you don't have to drive to find it, either. Corporate websites and corporate Facebook pages are rich resources of information, which not only identify a company's major areas of interest and innovation but, typically, they also list principal managers, with contact information. Another great resource is the annual report. All publicly traded companies publish annual reports for their shareholders. You can find these on the website of any publicly traded company.

Target key industry organizations—including, if appropriate, the local chamber of commerce—for membership. Sometimes it takes a bit of research to identify the appropriate organizations, and sometimes it just takes a fortunate exercise in networking. For many years, the late power broker Dan Sweat was one of the most important and respected public servants in Atlanta. One day, I found myself at an event in which I was in the same room with him and a few other people. I approached him.

"Mr. Sweat," I said, "I'm Ricky Steele from Columbus, Georgia."

"Oh, I know who you are, Ricky!"

"I've been in Atlanta a couple of years, and I know you're one of the real power brokers here. I'd give anything to come over to your office and chat with you for twenty minutes."

"Name the time."

I called him the next day, went over to visit with him, and told him about my limousine business and what I was trying to accomplish with it. "If I could have a mentor like you," I said, "I could go ten times farther than I'll ever go on my own."

"Ricky, I don't know how I can help you, but maybe there is one thing. As you know, I am the executive director of Central Atlanta Progress, and we are an invitation-only organization."

Of course, I knew that, and I also knew the smallest member company was about a hundred times larger than mine.

Mr. Sweat then asked: "How would you like to join CAP?"

Minimum dues were $5,000, which, at the time, was way beyond anything I could pony up. I explained this.

"Well, why don't I waive your dues for the first year? We're having our annual meeting in a couple of weeks, and I want you to come as my guest."

I was on my way! As a member of CAP, I met people I never would have met otherwise. The next time I went to a meeting, people were asking, "So, did you get my card?"

Did Dan Sweat have to do this for me? Of course not. Did I now "owe" him? He surely never let on that he thought I did. He never called me for any quid pro quo or favor for the rest of his life, which ended much too early in 1997. He could have said, "Ricky, shut your company down for the next two weeks and come over and do my yard work," and I would have done it. Dan never asked. Dan moved from CAP a number of years later to become the executive director of the Americas Project for President Carter. Dan used his influence to help me start a non-profit, "Hospitality Helping Hands," in partnership with Hands on Atlanta and then helped secure President Carter as a speaker for a convention I was chairing. A simple handshake and one meeting helped change Atlanta and me forever. Never forget the power of one good friend.

Be There

Dan was a mover and a shaker. If I hadn't done my homework, I wouldn't have recognized him when I saw him, and I wouldn't have targeted him for conversation. If I hadn't talked with him, my network would have been much, much smaller than it became as soon as I started circulating in CAP. There's a reason movers and shakers are called by that name. Meeting the right one can put a whole lot into motion. Maybe you remember something from your high school chemistry. I hope so because an analogy comes to mind. Meeting most people is like an ordinary chemical reaction. You meet, you interact, and, if all goes well, something happens between you. You make a sale, you make a good contact, or maybe you even make a friend. Meeting a mover and shaker, however, is more like a nuclear reaction. The exchange between the two of you doesn't affect just you and the other person; it has a far-reaching, highly energetic effect. Under the right circumstances, such a contact initiates a chain reaction, and your network explodes—in a wonderful way.

That's what happened to me when my connecting with Dan Sweat, a mover and shaker, put me into CAP. Again, high school chemistry. A chain reaction requires not only a mover and a shaker, but the presence of many other movers and shakers. Scientists call this a "critical mass." And that is precisely what CAP events offered. As a result, my network expanded rapidly and productively.

The savvy networker makes it his or her business to identify the organizations and the events most likely to offer a critical mass of movers and shakers. How many events are we talking about? That depends on where you are and what you do for a living. Before Covid-19, It was not unusual for me, on a given day, to attend two or three breakfast meetings, two lunches, a dinner, a reception, plus some other nightly event. Even when the pandemic has slowed its roll, at my age and what I focus on now, I will probably never be as active as I was from 1975 to 2015, but had I not done it over my forty prime years, I would not have experienced the success in business or in the not-for-profit world. In those days, I did all this—and it *is* a lot—to see the people who are important to me, whether I was going to sell them something on that particular day or ever. I did this to learn something, and I did this just to enjoy the companionship of people I like.

If you're new to a city, find people who will tell you where the good meetings are for your area of interest. If you're new to networking, go to as many meetings as you possibly can. One size does not fit all, and the group that proves to be a productive networking ground for your friend may not necessarily yield good contacts for you. Keep trying and keep attending. It's worth the time and effort.

If I were about to move to a new city and decided to give myself a single year to build a network, I'd spend the last week or ten days in my old place aggressively networking with the many people I know. I'd go see as many friends as I could, and I'd ask them, "Who do you know in New Town? Would you mind sending some e-mails on my behalf?"

My hope would be that these folks would transmit such messages as, "Hey, John, you've never met a guy like Ricky Steele. He's aggressive. He is hard working. He is committed. He is a community leader. Atlanta is going to miss him, but our loss is your gain. If you give him fifteen minutes to tell you who he is when he gets to town, I promise that you'll be reading about him in the New Town papers within a year."

I would make certain to get a list of the recipients of my friends' e-mails and, using this list, send e-mails of my own to this effect: "Dear John. I'm a good friend of Bill Smith, and I'm moving to your city next week with my company. I'll be new to the area, but I'm really excited about what I can offer your community. I'm deeply involved in volunteerism, especially in the areas of hunger and homelessness. I'm also involved in community redevelopment through volunteers, and I would appreciate a few minutes of your time."

Once I made the move, I'd set about meeting with whomever I could by using networking contacts, by volunteering, and by joining community organizations. I'd start reading the local business journals and the local newspapers. Soon, I'd be well on my way toward achieving my one-year networking goal.

Just as you keep a database of all your individual contacts, replete with as much biographical information as you can garner, you need to keep a file on every event in town. Who are the officers in the organization behind the event? Who are the players in attendance? What is the stated purpose of the event? Why do the movers and shakers attend? Is it strictly a networking event, or is it the weekly, monthly, or quarterly meeting of an affinity group? Diligently track the event, the frequency of meetings, membership, average number of attendees, program, format, and, not least of all, the price of admission. Some events are free, while some come with an admission fee of $100, $500, $1,000, or maybe as much as $10,000. Some events are open to the public, whereas others are open to members only or by invitation only.

Examine your event database and, using it, narrow down to your target events. Think in terms of value rather than price. A high-ticket event likely to be attended by the people you need to meet is a much better value than a free event attended by a couple hundred other service providers and job seekers. The hard fact is that, except for not-for-profit meetings, events I pay to attend are typically more productive than events that don't charge dues or fees. Some events are worth their weight in gold.

For instance, for those working in the technology sector in Atlanta, the Atlanta CEO Council, https://atlantaceo.org, is the best of the best. It was started over twenty years ago by a group of dedicated, very smart, and very successful technology leaders with the purpose of giving emerging growth technology companies a place to exchange ideas and hear great programs without being bombarded by a room filled with job seekers and service providers.

There were and there still are a lot of organizations that provide these sorts of event, and often these are free or very inexpensive. The Council meets once every six weeks, and each event is filled with early to mid-stage companies and large, more successful company executives who were once part of the organization when their businesses were at a very early stage, perhaps even pre-revenue companies.

I have been a member of The Council since the very beginning, twice as an entrepreneur with my own software company and as an employee with Definition 6. However, more often than not, I or the company I worked for paid for membership including PwC, Korn/Ferry, and now with Talent 360 Solutions. The beauty of the Council is that paid membership is restricted to just three service providers per category, whether it is lawyers, accountants, or staffing companies. Most other organizations do not limit attendance in that way, so you can often be in a room with more service providers than potential clients, and there may be ten or more of your competitors in the room all fighting to get and hold the attention of potential clients. Because of the Council's restriction, the value of being a member of something like the Atlanta CEO Council is more than recuperated by the value of being included.

What is the price to join the Atlanta CEO Council as a service provider? Ten thousand dollars per year, and worth every penny because it is just plain and simple good!

Look Beyond the Obvious

Industry organizations and events are the obvious stomping grounds of the networker. Be there, for sure, but also look beyond the obvious. I am a big believer in volunteering my time and contributing financially to causes that are important to me, my family, friends, clients, and prospects. Even if you are not able to contribute financially, everyone can volunteer an hour to feed the hungry, visit the sick, help clean a park and the list goes on and on.

In Atlanta, we have Hands on Atlanta, https://www.handsonatlanta.org, an amazing organization for which I have been volunteering for more than thirty years. I cannot share in this book all of the positive experiences I have personally experienced because of my volunteering at HOA, United Way, TechBridge, Atlanta Community Food Bank, Real Men Wear Pink for Breast Cancer, and other not-for-profit organizations.

Starting in 2006, I was the Host and Moderator of a CIO panel discussion for the United Way of Atlanta Technology Initiative. Each year, we would pick four prominent CIOs and host a breakfast where we would invite companies to meet them and hear what keeps them up at night while also discussing why they are involved with United Way. We raised tens of thousands of dollars over the years, and I met some incredible folks along the way. I could tell stories about almost all the CIOs, but I'll tell you about meeting Mr. William T. "Bill" VanCuren, the CIO of NCR.

Bill was a panelist in the year or two after NCR relocated from Ohio to Atlanta. I had met him briefly earlier and had heard him speak. He is a tall man with an even taller name in our community. After the event, I gave a copy of an earlier edition of this book to each panelist. Several months passed before I ran into Bill at the Inspire CIO of the Year Award presentation, where his CEO at the time, Mr. Bill Nuti, was the guest speaker. At the end of that program, I helped escort Mr. Nuti to a separate part of the facility to do a Q&A with all the CIOs who had attended. Standing in the back, Bill said to me, "I have been meaning to call you to tell you that I read your book and enjoyed it.

Coming from Ohio, my values and yours are very similar. I would love to go to lunch with you at some point to get to know you better."

I thought I had won the lottery! A potential client for a Fortune 250 company is asking me to lunch.

"I am open today, let's go now," I said, chomping at the bit.

He informed me that today did not work, but his assistant would set it up for a later date. That later date soon arrived, and I did my usual research and friendly stalking of Bill and his family. I learned a great deal about them and how special they all were. During lunch, we talked mostly about family, beliefs, principles, and everything but business. A friendship was created. It would take me two more books to explain everything that happened after that lunch, but since then, I have spent a lot of time with one of his sons, who was a student at University of Georgia. I shared with him my networking tips and later made an introduction that opened a door to an internship with a company in Atlanta. It worked because after college, his first job was for that company. I invited another son, who was attending Auburn, to an event where Dan Cathy spoke and all the Chick-fil-A sandwiches he could eat and take back to Auburn were available.

Bill's mom and his wife both became Facebook friends. I am very fond of his wife, whom I first met at a TechBridge Digital Ball, and we have also sorted food together at the Atlanta Community Food Bank. I don't think there is anything unusual about this story at all. This is a story about what can happen when two people become friends and how that meeting can improve hundreds of thousands of lives in our community as a result.

At some point in our relationship, I invited Bill to come sort food with us at the Food Bank. He had never visited it before, although he was already a regular volunteer with TechBridge, Women in Technology, the United Way, and a number of other not-for-profit organizations. After his first visit, Bill began inviting his iNCRedible technology team members to join him at the Food Bank each month. Often at our food-sorting events, 25 to 30 percent of our entire volunteer group are NCR team members or, as I like to call them, "The i**NCR**edibles."

When Covid-19 shut down schools, Bill worked with other NCR leaders to open their corporate kitchen, which was closed (together with their home office) due to the pandemic. NCR volunteered its use to prepare meals for children who normally received breakfast and lunch at school each day. Thousands of children did not go to bed hungry because of his passion to make the world a better place for all God's children. Finally, and this is the "over and above" gift that keeps on giving, Bill and his wife, Jeannie became regular financial givers to the Atlanta Community Food Bank giving our Food Bank the financial support to feed even more hungry neighbors.

The bottom line of this story about two men who became friends runs far deeper than business. Bill volunteered, the work resonated with him, and the result is that over 500,000 men, women, and children have received at least one meal over the past six years because of a United Way panel discussion ten years ago that opened the door for great things to follow. Bill will always remain a friend and inspiration to me.

I've been volunteering for most of my life, first in church, later in high school with the Junior Jaycees while growing up in Columbus, and in many other groups since then. It has always felt good to give, and I've stayed with it. The bonus of doing good can be doing well, and I've been blessed to build a great volunteer network of community-minded businesspeople. By volunteering, I've met a lot of people I would never have met in any other venue, among them the living legend Muhammad Ali, who once said, "Service to others is the rent you pay for your room here on earth."

Volunteer, and it is impossible to give more than you receive. The returns are fantastic! First and foremost is the deep satisfaction of giving. In addition, you reap the rewards of standing beside somebody who is not only passionate about the same things you are, but is also clearly an involved, committed businessperson, one who, very likely, works at a company about which you want to know more.

Volunteering also provides a marvelously non-threatening, low-pressure networking environment. You're shoveling dirt, painting a house, building steps for senior citizens, serving food—doing a hundred different things that make a difference—and, in the course of this work, the conversation will turn to more than the grade of the steps or the proportion of sand in the cement. You'll talk about your kids, about what you do, about where you work, and about what you have to offer. You'll open the door to a relationship.

Once that door is open, it's up to you to decide how far to step through it. You may be asked to serve on the board of the non-profit, and, if you accept, you will find yourself seated at a table with other volunteers who came up through the ranks as well as with CEOs and company vice-presidents, the key people you need to meet, the key people who will discover that, like them, you are deeply committed to the community you all share.

It is not hard to get started in volunteer work. Identify something about which you're passionate, and then find out how to get involved, whether it's adult literacy, feeding the homeless, mental health issues or marching for civil and human rights—whatever is needed, you can fill that need. The possibilities, and the returns, are endless as you find yourself among the proverbial pillars of your community.

I have met hundreds of great people, from executives to hourly employees, through volunteering. Everyone is equal, especially when everyone is giving of themselves. I met Tom while I was on the board of the Atlanta Community Food Bank. Tom had recently left First National Bank of Atlanta (today Wells Fargo) and was now consulting for banks around the country. We spent quite some time together, and I thoroughly enjoyed meeting him. Several years later, after we were no longer were on the board together, Tom accepted a senior position with Equifax, eventually becoming chairman and CEO. I did not call him often, but the few times I did, he always returned my calls within a day or two. I could work the rest of my life to meet someone with the stature, integrity, and success of a Tom Chapman and still not come close. A lucky "chance" meeting? I think not. Tom's retired now, so we will probably never do business together again. Doesn't matter. I am proud to tell anyone who will listen that I have a relationship with him.

Networking is all about community, whether it's the community of business or the community at large. In addition to non-profit volunteer organizations, you can make contact with the community through participation in various civic organizations and institutions, the most common of which, for most people, is their child's school. Some of your most effective networking contacts can be made in this venue. Who are the parents of your child's friends? What businesses are they in? Don't sit quietly at PTA or PTO meetings or school committee meetings. Don't stand on the sidelines at soccer games as if you're on the edge of a leper colony. Network!

"Hi, I'm Ricky Steele."

"I'm John Jones."

"Are you *the* John Jones at Widgets Unlimited? My daughter has told me how smart your son is. We ought to get to know each other a bit better."

My agenda? Just to get to know him a little bit better and, in return, to let him know that I'm a serious businessman, who might just have something to offer him.

The savvy networker identifies the key people and the must-attend events, but he or she also looks beyond the obvious and seizes on every opportunity to expand a growing network. In the next chapter, we'll get even more specific about how to connect with the people who can most productively build your network.

4

■

Strategy and Tactics

IN THE LAST CHAPTER, WE CONSIDERED SOME OF THE PREPARATION that is essential to positioning yourself to meet the movers and shakers who should become part of your network. In this chapter, I share the strategy and tactics that have worked well for me to ensure that, once I am positioned for a meeting, I can follow through to make the meeting a reality.

The Early Bird . . .

At a conference or a seminar, I often walk up to an acquaintance, put my hand out, and say, "Hey, Joe Jehoshaphat! How're you doing? What's been going on with the Widget Company?"

The response, invariably, is something like, "Gosh, Ricky, you *are* unbelievable with names! How do you do it?"

I just smile by way of reply and keep shaking that hand, all the time thinking to myself, *The reason I remember your name is because I was here an hour ago scanning the name badges on the registration table!*

At most events, name badges are laid out on a table for registrants to pick up as they file in. Many people like to work at the office as late as possible, rush to a scheduled event fifteen or twenty minutes tardy and be considered fashionably late. I can appreciate the need to finish another project or two, but if you are not serious about the upcoming event, stay at the office and make sure your project is picture perfect. My goal is to arrive at least fifteen to thirty minutes *early* for any event—and not just to scan the name badges. (Though this is *very* important!)

I start by talking to the registration people. I have developed many friendships over the years with some fine people many folks never take the time even to make eye contact with, let alone meet and talk to. I volunteer to help them in any way I can, whether it is arranging the name tags or putting material on each table or chair. I have moved podiums and rearranged the seating at the last minute because the organizer did not have time to wait for the hotel staff to make the changes they needed. Giving this help doesn't cause me to break much of a sweat, and it allows me to get to know the event coordinators and meeting planners much better. I want them to know that I recognize the value of what they do. Meeting planning and event coordination are much more than ordering finger sandwiches and booze.

I once heard Ambassador Andrew Young speak to a group of meeting planners, which, at the time, included me. Andy started his speech by telling us how much he appreciated our jobs and how he had been a meeting planner earlier in life. I am not sure if any of us believed Andy until he explained, "I was Martin Luther King, Jr.'s meeting planner. I booked the hotels, arranged the cars, ordered the food, and made the airline reservations." I don't know how much any of us digested from the rest of Andy's presentation as we left the room. I was joined by many others in awestruck tears as we contemplated this fellow servant in God's world.

I sometimes forget to make a reservation, or my schedule opens up at the last minute, and I find that I can attend something I did not register in advance to attend. How often do you think I am asked to pay a late registration fee? Almost never. It's not because I do not deserve to pay the fee, but because I have been granted favor and given grace by a friend in hospitality who knows I would not take advantage of them in any way.

Once I finish any chores given to me, I try to spend as much time as possible scanning the name badges—without holding up any lines or getting in the way of the table staff. Once the attendees begin arriving, it is time for me to step aside. Many times, I have not gotten to the end of the row of badges. Because of good relationships with many planners, I've been able to obtain from them a copy of the entire registration list. I scan it discreetly on the spot and, once finished, immediately give it back to my friend.

Why do I scan the badges or the lists? I have always had trouble with names. My dad was horrible as well. He usually was able to come up with the names of his children but most everyone else was "Friend," "Good Buddy," "Brother," or "Sister." As a networker and public speaker, I have the pleasure of meeting many people. I can remember faces fairly well, but until we have broken bread together or spent real time getting to know each other, I usually have to dig hard to come up with a name. Scanning the name badges or a registration list beforehand helps me put names with the faces I see. I can watch people arrive and be able to come up with names because I have been expecting them to be there. This is not a foolproof system, but it is better than any other I have tried.

One of my most embarrassing moments occurred many years ago now, but it has stuck with me because it was so embarrassing. Atlanta's foundational technology guru and the technology partner at Morris Manning and Martin, one of the city's premier law firms, is John Yates. I am also blessed to call John a dear friend. Once, John invited me to an event at his office with about thirty venture capitalists. I was the only service provider present. I met a new VC from North Carolina for the first time as I was walking through the front door. We spoke briefly but were interrupted within seconds. I got a cup of coffee, moved to the opposite side of the room, and began talking to another group of Atlanta venture capitalists. Suddenly, I saw someone walking toward me. I knew I knew him. I remembered we had met briefly once and had talked a little about his company, but I panicked because I could not remember his name.

When he got within speaking and reaching distance, I stuck out my hand and said, "Hello, my name is Ricky Steele."

He looked at me with the most peculiar expression and said, "I know. We just met on the other side of the conference table."

I wanted to melt into the carpet but came back weakly with my usual quip, "I knew that, but I did not know if you would remember me." I doubt he bought for a second my attempt at a comeback, and I was now more embarrassed for being willing to lie to cover my loss of memory.

Now, I promise that I am about to share with you a few hard-learned lessons on avoiding this kind of embarrassment while also adding to your network. But first, I want to explain why my embarrassment on this occasion was so painful. The reason is simple: the gaffe happened at an event I attended only because John Yates had thought of *me*—had remembered *me*—and invited *me*. It was a valuable invitation, and I felt I had disrespected it and, in so doing, disrespected my friend.

To understand the scope of my embarrassment, you have to appreciate what kind of person John Yates is. To convey to you that appreciation, I first need to tell an important networking story.

As a passionate volunteer for many organizations over the years, I have had many unique and amazing opportunities. In the 1980s, I served for six years on the International Board of Meeting Professionals International. Because I was in the Destination Management industry, I was viewed as a "Supplier," in contrast to Meeting Planners for The Coca-Cola Company, IBM, AT&T, and the National Association of Home Builders, who were regarded as the Professionals." Suppliers like me attended the meetings and volunteered to meet more of the Professionals because they were the ones who gave us business. I duly volunteered and paid my own way to attend many conventions across the USA and to serve on the Membership Committee. Once, I even served on the Selection Committee when we were looking for a new CEO. As a result of my hard work and commitment, I was finally asked to serve on the International Board, consisting of roughly fifty people out of the 10,000 members.

Having served on twenty-plus not-for-profit boards over the years, I can say without a doubt that MPI was the most rewarding. In addition to Board meetings held in the States, we met every other year internationally, including amazing trips to Hong Kong, London, and Montreux, Switzerland. Because each city that hosted our meetings also wanted to showcase their town to the Professionals in the organization, we were always flown First Class, stayed in huge, luxury suites, and wined and dined like I had not experienced before or since. It was fun, I admit, but I worked hard.

Playing a role in organizations like MPI positioned me for other roles that were deeply meaningful and rewarding in themselves, but also enlarged my own network within the industries I served and the broader community we all served. On one occasion, I was asked to chair the United Way Technology Initiative. Perhaps second only to my work with MPI, this was the most prestigious opportunity with which I've ever been presented in my professional career. It promised to expose me to senior level executives that I would not otherwise likely meet, but the most immediate task at hand was to bring together as many senior-level technology executives as possible to promote the United Way and to raise money.

I was thrilled and deeply honored to be asked to accept this role, but I did not jump at the offer. I promised to think about it and deliver my decision very soon. I thought that if I had a few days of mentally lying to myself, I could convince myself that I was capable of doing the job. I knew what the job would mean in recognition for me personally and for my company.

Thought about it? I *wrestled* over it. At the end of wrestling with myself, I tapped out. I finally realized that the real opportunity I was being offered was the opportunity to do the right thing.

The question was, What was the right thing?

I knew the answer. It was to recommend someone else to be the chairperson. Would it have looked good on my resume to chair this effort? Would it have opened doors to new business? Would it garner for me press coverage in the *Atlanta Business Chronicle* and the *Atlanta Journal-Constitution* as the Chairman of this Initiative? Without a doubt. But, led by me, would the effort have been as successful as it would have been under someone more distinguished, experienced, and relevant in the Atlanta tech industry? Without a doubt, no.

I knew what would be best. Ethically, there was no other choice I could make. Until this moment in time, I have never shared this story with another living soul including the person who accepted the role.

And that brings us back to John Yates.

I don't know who said it first, but it is true: "There is no limit to what you can accomplish if you do not care who gets the credit." Once I made my decision, I did not have to wrestle myself or anyone else to decide that John Yates was *the* ideal person to chair this initiative. Very few people have had as much to do with the success of Atlanta and Georgia as a growing technology community. I can think of none who have done more.

I can't list John's accomplishments because I can't afford to pay for the extra page count in this book. Just google "John Yates" or visit his LinkedIn profile. One thing about John that I knew then and I know today is that he is a very busy man. He is famous for three business breakfasts at the same restaurant—not back-to-back, as I have been known to do over the years—but simultaneously. John does not miss a beat at any of them, in spite of jumping in and out of each breakfast between courses. John is also an avid volunteer along with his wife, Ellen. They have done so very much to fight childhood cancer and to grow the Decatur Family YMCA.

So, I was a bit daunted. What could I do or say to John that would encourage him to get involved with another time-intensive program for a not-for-profit organization? This is where doing your homework and engaging your network come in. I knew that Mr. Kent "Oz" Nelson, Chairman of the Board of UPS, was also the volunteer Chairman of the Board of United Way of Greater Atlanta that year. I asked the person at the United Way who asked me to be the Chair if he thought that he could get Mr. Nelson to call John personally to talk about the opportunity. I did not know if John already knew Mr. Nelson or whether he or his firm were doing any business with UPS. However, I did know that Mr. Nelson was an icon in the Atlanta business community, and I was sure that anyone who did not know him would appreciate the opportunity to meet him.

A few days later, it was arranged. I called John and made my pitch about the committee and, at the end, said, "Would you have the time to take a call from Oz Nelson, Chairman of UPS to discuss this further"?

I will share no more about our conversation except for this: John was the first Chairman of the United Way's Technology Initiative. He founded its success. It raised more money than had been projected and substantially increased the visibility of United Way into the technology community. The United Way of Greater Atlanta created the "John Yates Community Service Award," which was given at the final meeting of John's year as Chairman.

Now, I promised that I would offer some advice to help you avoid the embarrassment of forgetting a person you met moments earlier. It is this: never stop networking. Do it in the moment (as I should have done at the conference) and do it over the long term. Part of the reason I was able to persuade John Yates to take on a major volunteer assignment was that I didn't try to persuade him on my own. I engaged my network.

It is important that you have a list of people within each industry or vertical market you are attempting to penetrate. You should have their names and a little something about them in your mental contact list. If you are scanning the name badge table and see one of your names, you now have an important task ahead of you. If you don't know the person on sight, you can wait by the table to see who picks up the badge. You can also search through your memory or, even better, search LinkedIn on your cell phone for the name of someone else at the event who is already connected with the person you want to meet. If you don't have a match, take the time to visit with others you know at the event and casually mention that you have been trying to meet so-and-so for several months and so far have not been successful.

"I think I remember you telling me you were friends with him. Am I remembering that correctly?"

If the answer is yes, ask for an introduction. Many times, I have had my friend look around the room and say, "Ricky, he is right over there. Let's go and meet him now before he is swamped with others seeking his attention."

An introduction from a mutual friend is heaven-sent. All you really want your friend to do is facilitate the introduction. Your goal is the introduction only. If you even dream you will sell something in the middle of a crowded ballroom within the first five minutes, you do not need to be reading this book. A better choice might be *Alice in Wonderland.* It is impossible to develop a meaningful relationship and really get to know someone on your first or second meeting. I have been acquainted with people for twenty years, and I really don't think I know them all that well. I am aware of what they sell or buy, but I don't know what makes them tick. I don't know what their real struggles are in their business or in their lives away from work.

If I cannot find someone to make the introduction, I rely on boldness. I slowly make my move to where my prospect is standing, I stick out my big hand, and I say, "Hello! I am Ricky Steele, I have heard a lot about you. As a matter of fact, I have tried calling you a few times, but I understand how busy you are."

If I've done my homework, I will be able to approach with at least one compelling fact at my fingertips.

"I read about your leadership on the United Way campaign. Congratulations on exceeding your goal. This is a wonderful reception and certainly not the place to talk business. Would you give me permission to call your assistant tomorrow and schedule a fifteen-minute visit in the next two weeks? I have some information that you may find helpful."

I can't remember when anyone has refused this request. I have not kissed my prospect's ring, nor have I approached him in a needy kind of way, but I have let him know that I recognize he is very busy and that his time is at a premium. I have also flattered him by demonstrating that I know something about him and his business. I've told him that I have information he may find helpful, and I have pledged to take no more than fifteen minutes of his time at *his* convenience. The best part: I've done all this in less than two minutes flat.

But there are also other reasons to get to a meeting early enough to scan the name badges. Not only do I learn who's going to be in attendance, so that I can make a mental list of the people I absolutely must try to see, I also have an opportunity to identify the time wasters, people to be avoided.

What I've just said sounds harsh, I know, and I'll explain myself on this point in just a little bit, but before I do, there is yet another reason to get to an event early. It gives you a chance to meet people you otherwise would not encounter. Most organizations have a board meeting before the regular meeting. By the time the board adjourns, the regular meeting has yet to begin, and if you are early—in the right place at the right time—you'll have an opportunity to see the movers and shakers as they emerge from their special meeting. These are the people you definitely want to meet.

A number of years ago, I had a conversation with my dear friend Mark Hersh. Mark is another community servant leader through his volunteer activities at the Roswell United Methodist Church "Job Seeker" program. He's also an all-around wonderful human being. Mark has heard me speak a number of times over the years. After one of those meetings, Mark proceeded to tell me this story.

"I want you to know that arriving at meetings early really works," he told me. "A couple months ago I was at a meeting where [Georgia's then-governor] Sonny Perdue was the keynoter. I arrived early and was scanning name badges. The governor walked up with an aide only to find out that his secretary had given him an incorrect arrival time, and he had an hour to wait before he spoke."

Governor Perdue and Mark had a chance to chat for ten minutes about technology in Georgia. Later that evening, the governor delivered his speech, on technology in Georgia. During the Q & A that followed, someone asked him a question about an issue he and Mark had discussed earlier. After answering the question to the best of his ability, the governor continued: "That's my opinion, but if you will go ask the big guy in the bright yellow shirt, I can promise you he knows much more than I."

The endorsement and exposure were great for Mark, and he was swamped after the meeting was concluded. New relationships resulted because Mark decided he was going to work smarter.

"That would never have happened in a million years had it not been for me learning that from your speech," Mark told me.

The moral? Next time, arrive early and see what doors open!

Make a Plan and Stay the Course

Now for the harsh reality. After I've scanned the name badges, I lay out in my head a strategy for the evening. Everyone at the meeting is important, but time is a scarce resource, and not everyone at that meeting represents a productive investment of my time. Just as I wouldn't squander my company's funds, I am not going to misappropriate my company's time. This is a business event, and if my company is paying me to attend it, I scan the name badges not only for the names of people I want to meet, but also for those I want to avoid.

I am much better at avoiding people if I know they're going to be attending and I can keep my eye on them. I'm not very good at avoiding them if they take me by surprise and manage to corner me. When cornered, however, I try my hardest to stay the course by moving on as quickly as possible.

I want to be kind to people because I'm committed to living out my faith, but I cannot do business if I allow my time to be dominated by any especially long-winded person. Even a single event is too precious to lose, and, even worse, if I let myself stray from strategy on one evening, chances are it will happen again and again. Therefore, as important as it is to identify and seek those with whom I must network, it is almost equally important to identify and avoid those that are not part of my goal for that evening. We can always get together at another time.

Depending on the nature of the event, the criteria for the people to avoid may vary. In general, however, I avoid the following:

- People who haven't learned the art of brevity. I always steer clear of anyone likely to tell me the history of Swiss watch making when I ask what time it is. I'm here to meet as many must-see people as possible. Where time is concerned, I'm on a tight budget.

- People who pontificate on their worth to the human race. Such folk are so immersed in themselves that they suck the air right out of the room. If a particular air-sucker happens to own a big business and is known for spending a million dollars a year in my area, I'll be tempted to learn to live on a little less air. Maybe I'll stand and listen. Otherwise, I do what I can to keep my all-too-scarce time from being monopolized.

- People who offer neither business nor opportunity to help me advance my company. These people may be great conversationalists, but I'm being paid to be at this meeting for one purpose only. Maybe we can get together socially on another, non-business, occasion.

- People whose agendas differ from mine. I don't want to spend time with anybody who is opinionated about things I have no interest in having a conversation about at this time. Politics, social issues, cousin's recent gall bladder operation. All these are important, but I'm being paid (or paying myself) to be at this meeting to do business. I cannot afford to misappropriate my company's time.

- People I'm not prepared to hold a conversation with at that moment. It takes self-discipline to avoid people you *could* do business with but with whom, *at the moment*, you are not prepared to speak productively. If I see a potential customer, but haven't done any research about them, their company, or their industry, if I can hardly pronounce the name of the technology they use, I know that contact at this time will benefit neither them nor me. I'll make a mental note of such people, and, if I want to pursue a connection later, I'll do my homework before the next event.

If all of this sounds judgmental, that's because it is! But it's a business judgment rather than a social judgment. I don't avoid people at business events because I think they're bad or dull people. I avoid them because I have only so much time to invest on this specific occasion.

I must admit the one subject I *will* always pause to discuss is my faith. Sometimes, people have even scheduled meetings with me to discuss this very topic. I always take the meeting, and I have been fooled a few times, arriving for the meeting only to discover that faith was not really their agenda item. So what? I do not have all the answers, but I do believe that the love that comes from God is available to every one of us. And outside of a business context, well, I'll talk to just about anyone, with the exception of those who are profane, shallow, or vindictive.

Try as I might, of course, I can't simply avoid everyone I need to avoid, and as much as I want to do business, I don't want to do it at the cost of offending anyone. If someone approaches me who isn't part of that evening's strategy to meet potential clients, I take proactive measures. "Bill," I'll say, "I've been trying to get with John Smith at the Widget Company forever. As soon as he walks in the door, Anne will introduce me to him. I hope this doesn't offend you, but I'm going to hang over there closer to her for the next few minutes, and when I get that accomplished, can we finish up later this evening? Or why don't we have lunch one day next week? I'd really like to hear what you've been up to."

Bill will understand. Most likely, he'll reply, "You know, we haven't had lunch for a while. Why don't we do that? My treat."

Bill is important to me, but so is my agenda for tonight, the things I have to accomplish this evening. Sure, I want to spend time with Bill, but now is not the right time. The fact is that most people are not offended when you are honest with them. What *is* offensive is your standing there talking to someone while your eyes intently scan the room for someone "more important." Everyone deserves your full attention. The strategy for this evening may demand that you give Bill your full attention *at another time*. Be honest about that. Not only will Bill understand, but he may also help you get connected with the person you need to talk with that evening.

Wrong Target

If I've done my homework, I know who has the power and authority to do business with me. I know who the buyers are in a company.

Those who aren't buyers don't make it onto my mental list to begin with, but it has happened on occasion that I've gotten to a meeting in a prospect's office and realized I had made a mistake. Either I wasn't meeting with the buyer, as I had thought, or this person was not interested in buying what I had to sell.

If he tells me that he's not the buyer and that John Smith is, I respond positively: "I've heard of him. He's a great guy. Would it be an imposition if I asked you to introduce me to John?"

"No, not at all. Let's walk over there right now."

After I'm introduced, John usually says, "Well, I guess I can give you a couple of minutes."

John is trying to be polite, but he's not really prepared to talk with me, which means he's not really prepared to consider buying from me. I don't want a little piece of his attention on the spur of the moment. I want his *full* attention when it is more convenient for him.

"No," I'll say, "I wasn't trying to get any of your time right now. I just had a terrific fifteen minutes with Bill, and he thought this would be a great introduction. Could I call your secretary tomorrow and ask her for fifteen or twenty minutes of your time sometime in the next couple of weeks?"

With relief, he'll exclaim, "Oh yeah! Of course."

I have just won a friend by turning down the opportunity to force myself through his door and hold him captive when he has nine crises, two projects past deadline, and a board meeting in an hour. He *had* to see me, because one of his colleagues brought me in. But I rescued him by letting him off the hook. A great networker is always trying to make it easy for the other person, and a planned meeting is always much easier than an ambush.

Offer Value Right Away

A pessimist would look at what I've just described and conclude that I had wasted my time. Not only had I spent fifteen minutes with the wrong person, I failed to seize the moment for a meeting with the right one. Now I'll have to take the extra time to make a return trip.

I don't look at it this way. Correcting my "mistake" gave me a positive opportunity to begin a relationship with my intended prospect by offering him value. By refusing to ambush John, I've made his life easier. That is a valuable gift to him. Ultimately, the basis of all business relationships is the offer of value in return for value received. This is the definition of a fair deal or a square deal or just plain good business. The earlier and more clearly you signal that you are here to give, not just take, the more likely it is that a full-scale, productive business relationship will develop over time.

When I'm at a conference, my company is paying me, and although I might want to spend most of my time with the people I already know—I'm comfortable with them—I'm paid to make new contacts with people who might be interested in the services my company has to offer. So, I am a firm believer in the importance of eating with strangers, and when I'm hunting for a seat at dinner, I deliberately avoid the table full of people from my own company.

"Sit with us!" they'll say.

"I know you all! How many of you at this table are going to buy something from me?"

In the mid-1980s, I was the founder and CEO of the largest destination management company in the Southeast. We had a staff of about 150 hard-working men and women. Our sales and marketing staff totaled fourteen people. Many times we would send eight to ten salespeople to cover major industry events. I had very few rules because I believed we had hired competent adults, who were smart enough to do the right thing. But I was serious about *one* rule. If I attended the event and ever saw two of our people sitting at the same table, they knew they would be meeting with me the next morning for a little talk. Sometimes, I would ask them to spend quality time together in one of their offices and invite them to share every secret of the universe. I expected them to come out of that office knowing enough about each other so they would never feel the need to sit together at a meeting again.

Do the math: ten salespeople sitting at two tables with five other executives at each table is five new contacts per five of your salespeople.

Ten of your people sitting at ten different tables with nine other executives will give your company *ninety* new contacts and potential customers. Tell me that ninety new contacts aren't better than ten.

I must admit that I have to force myself to eat with strangers. It doesn't come naturally. But once I'm seated, I'm not uncomfortable, because I have a mission to focus on. I introduce myself, of course, but I spend the first several minutes of any conversation as a more-or-less silent listener. My task is to learn as much as I can about each of the people at the table and, during this, look for opportunities to offer value. For example, I learn from the drift of conversation that Sarah, a young African American woman seated across from me, is a principal in a fledgling biotech firm. The tumblers click in the back of my mind.

"Sarah," I speak up, "I heard the other day about a new program that is doing unique financing for minority-owned biomedical companies. I could put you in touch with someone who knows all about that program."

Now I'm offering value. Perhaps it will result in business between me and Sarah's firm. Maybe it will just connect her with the financing she needs, and I won't see a dime of business as a result. That's fine. A gift can't be offered on condition of payment. However, at the very least, I've demonstrated to Sarah and six other people at the table that I offer value, so that getting to know me might be a pretty good idea. In an instant, I'm no longer a stranger among strangers.

As the meal continues, other conversations begin. Pete, to my left, says, "I'm an Auburn Tiger fan. I graduated in 1992, my wife graduated a year later, and we've been Tiger fans forever." This information, together with other bits I gather this evening, will go into my database. It may never be worth a nickel to me, but, then again, it might.

If I get home from the meeting early enough, I try to input as much information as I can remember into my database right away. If I'm just too beat, I'll do it as soon as I get up the next morning. To aid my memory, I carry a little notepad with me and, discreetly, out of sight, scribble a few notes throughout the evening. However, if I wait two or three days to input stuff into my database, most of the scribbling will have ceased to make sense. I record everything while it is very fresh in my mind.

I also try to *do* something with the information as soon as I possibly can. Pete is in a business unrelated to mine, so I'm not going to be selling anything to him. But one of my best clients can offer a product that should interest Pete, and he happens to be a big-time Tiger fan with season tickets on the 50-yard line.

I get on the telephone: "Ted, it's Ricky. I met a Mr. Pete Jones last night, and he was the nicest guy. He's also an Auburn Tiger fan, who is in the widget business. I think he would be receptive to hearing about your company's line. I'll arrange lunch in the next two weeks with you, me, and Pete Jones. You can invite him to come down for the first game of the season."

Although there is no direct profit to me, by facilitating a relationship between Pete and my client, I reinforce and reaffirm my relationship with my current client while I simultaneously create a friend in Pete Jones. I benefit from both relationships precisely because I demonstrate that I am truly interested in helping these two people. I have revealed myself as the kind of guy most people want to do business with: generous and service oriented.

Another passion I have had for many years involves what almost every company needs more of: additional revenue. Without revenue, the best product, location, sales team, and celebrity endorsement will not keep the company from folding. One of my offers and something that has often been the difference between my being chosen over a competitor is my passion to put more revenue in my client's pocket than my company receives in fees.

Is this always possible?

No, but it is often doable if caring for your clients and their needs over your own is part of your value proposition. I make this offer to every client, and, in some cases, it has created multi-millions of dollars of new revenue for the client. I am convinced that the only reason that one of the companies I have worked with over the years received a Global Staffing Contract with Dell is because an introduction I made.

Who would believe that the multi-billion-dollar Dell does not already know everyone in their world? Well, after meeting with a Dell regional vice president and going over his prospect list, I was able to open several doors, one of which resulted in a multimillion-dollar transaction. You would think that a company that spends more on hand sanitizer each week than I have made in income over the last half-century would not need help penetrating any company in the world. Never be discouraged by what you assume. Take a chance.

After receiving a Global Staffing Contract, I was also invited to attend Dell World in Las Vegas. Pretty high cotton for a small-time sales guy out of Columbus, Georgia. Later, the first large client of a start-up security company for which we were recruiting happened when I introduced their CEO to the CEO of a Fortune 500 client at a Atlanta CEO Council Roundtable event at the Ritz Buckhead. Both companies spent millions of dollars with our firm because I was fortunate to be able to introduce two friends who I had spent years getting to know and magic happened between them. The key to success to me is to find as many ways as possible to help others succeed and many of them will do all they can to help *you* succeed.

Of course, I have failed to achieve this promise many times over the years because there are some companies that are too big and/or their sales process is not conducive to this sort of relationship building, but I was still able to do business with the company that I attempted to help because they appreciated the effort. Most of the additional stories in this edition of *The Heart of Networking* are not intended just to give myself a pat on the back. They are to encourage you to think outside the box. What can you do that is unique to your industry and prospect base? If you can afford the time and the expense, do that—and reap the rewards.

Sadly, no good idea lasts forever, so you have to keep adapting. In addition, anything you create that brings you success will be stolen by both your friends and your competitors, so you will have to customize yet again. However, the best ideas and tactics are often either hard to do or they require discipline and patience. You be the person that sticks to your plan long after your competitors quit using the idea because they did not see results in the first two hours after launching their version of your ideas. Bottom line: bring value, make your customers successful, support their efforts in the community through attendance and on social media. The more success they achieve, the more discretionary income they have to invest in your products and services. If you help generate that for them, they are not calling your competitor for bids when they have the need for your services because they are a little less expensive or offer better payment terms. You are their partner, not just their vendor.

Databasing

I've already mentioned more than a few times the importance of entering contact information into a database. Networking works best on a handshake and eye-to-eye basis, but some well-placed electronic intervention helps, too. All effective networkers need a system to store contact and client information. There are many contact-management software packages on the market today, including Outlook, Act, and Google Apps, among other, smaller brands. If you already own the hardware and the software, use it. If not, go online and read the reviews of experts and actual users. All the major contact-management products give you plenty of space to include every possible piece of information you can obtain about your contacts and customers. In addition to name, business address, e-mail, cell phone, home address, and relevant websites and presences on social networking sites (see Chapters 5, 6, and 7), you'll want to record the spouse's name and birthday, children's names and birthdays, the couple's anniversary date, high schools and colleges attended, and degrees earned. Also include data on fraternity or sorority, and athletics in high school, college, and now. I always record the contact's position in his company, his previous two employers, his assistant's name, and any private or business clubs he belongs to. I want to know his religious persuasion or lack thereof. And, yes, does he have season tickets to the local baseball, football, hockey, opera, symphony, or tractor pull events?

Of course, if you do not have the information in your database, try searching LinkedIn and Google. LinkedIn generally provides college, city currently residing, last three or four companies, and often links to information they shared with others or that they found helpful shared by others. Often, the subject of the article is not as important as knowing whose opinion/ideas they value. Google their name and then Google Mr. and Mrs. William Potential Client. They may live close to the vest and do not share a great deal of information on social media, but their spouse might, and this could include charities, colleges, house of worship, and information about their extended family. All pieces of gold lying in wait for you to claim.

A pile of information may look impressive sitting there, but it has little intrinsic value until you start analyzing, manipulating, and using it. That's why you need good contact software as opposed to, say, a plain old word processing program. The contact management software lets you sort data in dozens of ways, mixing and matching categories and people. Pete is an Auburn fan. Some time ago I met another Auburn fan. Who was it? I open up my contact manager and do an electronic search. Bingo! Another thing I know about Pete is that he's in the market for widget cleaners. Who among my contacts can supply his need? Search. *Yes!*

Six Degrees of Separation

In 1990, a play by John Guare curiously titled *Six Degrees of Separation* premiered on Broadway. It was made into a film in 1993 starring Donald Sutherland, Will Smith, and Stockard Channing. The idea behind the odd title is the proposition that anyone of us is separated from anyone else by no more than six degrees. The idea was so intriguing that some wag invented a parlor game called "Six Degrees of Kevin Bacon," in which players connect with that actor in six steps or less: Joe knows John, who knows Susie, who knows Ed, whose father went to school with Kevin Bacon's mother. The trick is to obtain the information that reveals the connections and delivers you to Kevin Bacon's figurative doorstep within six moves.

If this six-degree proposition sounds implausible to you, I know that it works. I promise you that I can connect with anyone in your universe within six steps if you make sufficient information available to me. That is what a database is for: cutting across the degrees of separation and making connections between apparent total strangers. How many of your contacts attended Harvard Business School? How many are lifelong Rotarians? How many play tennis or golf? These and other criteria are the degrees separating you from your potential latest customer or newest best friend.

I firmly believe that we are all just a few contacts away from meeting anyone we need to meet. The more information I have, the easier it will be for me to determine how to connect someone I want to know with someone I already know. Not only does this information help me make contacts, it also helps me make connections among my contacts, which humanize and facilitate my own relationships.

I believe, for instance, that I can connect anybody in the technology business in Atlanta with anybody else in the technology business in fewer than six steps. Bill Jones, a software executive I need to meet, is a graduate of Duke. Two of the members of my super-network group are also Duke graduates. With this information, I can start playing six degrees of separation to find someone who can introduce me to Bill Jones. That's why I have a lot of fields in my database. I cannot have too much information about anyone, whether it's the fact that they're left-handed or the fact that they played club field hockey in college. To connect the people, I need to connect the fields.

Let me give you an example of how this works. Back when I was a partner at Korn/Ferry, I was meeting with a local venture capitalist about one of his portfolio companies. I did some Internet research and found that he was a graduate of the University of North Carolina, got his MBA at Wharton, and was on the golf team in college. In our first meeting, I said, "You might find it interesting that two of my partners are also graduates of North Carolina."

"How did you know I was a graduate of North Carolina?" he asked.

I told him that I always do research before entering a meeting. Later I said, "One of my partners loves to play golf and is a member at both the new East Lake course as well as the Piedmont Driving Club. Do you still enjoy playing competitively?"

"I certainly do. I play in as many amateur tournaments as I can in addition to four or five charity golf tournaments annually. I have always wanted to play the new course at the Piedmont Driving Club.

"Let me check with Bill and see what we can do to make that possible."

When I got back to the office, I went immediately to Bill and offered (or maybe I begged) to caddy if he would take my VC friend out for a round. Bill agreed, and I put him in touch with my contact. At that point, they realized that they had, in fact, met before. All of a sudden, my connection had been humanized. The venture capitalist knew that I wasn't there just to hustle him, but that I wanted to get to know him. I was able to persuade him that I represented more than a one-shot transaction. I offered a genuine relationship, worth whatever time he might choose to invest in it.

This is the real objective of any valid networking strategy: to move from the status of stranger to a partner in a relationship, which may or may not result directly in business, but that, given time, will nevertheless prove productive. Executing the strategy begins with contact, information and—sometimes—progresses from one degree to the next until you've connected with your chosen prospect. However, just because you connect the dots that lead to your prospect does not oblige your prospect to connect with *you*. The next chapter considers networking obstacles and speed bumps, and it presents some tactics for rolling over them.

5

■

A Way of Being Online

I BOUGHT MY FIRST COMPUTER IN 1990 for the editor of a magazine I was publishing at the time. I don't remember the price, but at the time it seemed a king's ransom. After watching the editor work with it for a while, she asked me if I wanted to learn how to operate it. Although I saw that this machine was clearly making her life easier, I proudly announced that at thirty-eight years old, having never used a computer in my life, I believed I could make it to a ripe old age without needing to do so.

I've since learned that thinking before engaging the mouth makes a good deal of sense.

In 1993, I was recruited as the CEO of a media start-up. Everyone in our organization had a computer, of course, and not wanting to seem like the Luddite I was, I broke down and bought one. To me, the purchase was more for the benefit of my colleagues than myself.

Our company bought vintage dial-up Internet connectivity and dialed in at a blazing 1600 baud. We later made it to 3,200 and finally to a mind-blowing 9,600. My colleagues and I spent many afternoons going to lunch while a page loaded. Even when the Internet seemed practically magic in its ability to connect people and to relay information, dealing with the unearthly scream of the modem and the life-long load times was still infuriating. In my heart, I remained against all this nonsense, even if I was beginning to understand the practical benefits.

I am now on the backside of my career, having in September 2022 reached seventy years of age. I do not know how I lived the first twenty-five years of my working life as a computer illiterate. I'm admitting all of this to warn you that I came into the computer age kicking and screaming. My emergence into the social networking world was even more painful.

Social Networking: A Personal Overview

I did not suffer in solitude. We Baby Boomers adopted social networking at a funereal pace. There were several reasons for this. To begin with, we felt we had made it this far without having to try a new-fangled tactic. We also assumed that social networking was a frivolous trend for the young, we were intimidated by the technology itself, and we simply did not see the value of involving ourselves.

So much for not-so-ancient history. As of late summer 2022, while I write these words, most of my generation and older have embraced and many have moved far past where we first started. In fact, social networking has not only become the place to meet new people and network with decision makers across many industries, it serves as a valuable forum to seek and gather the opinion of others. It is like having your own private focus group any time you want one. I often pose a question on LinkedIn, Twitter, or Facebook to hear what others are thinking or how they may have handled a problem I am facing. Companies use social media to gauge interest in a new product, discover how the public feels about their customer service, or to seek new ideas or even new employees.

This is a freely available focus group—although maybe it's more accurate to call it "crowdsourcing." Either way, I find that many of the replies I receive are insightful. They provide me with new ways to look at an issue.

I'm hardly alone in this, of course. Social media influences everything, including every United States election since 2008, when Barack Obama raised awareness and millions of dollars through social media, becoming our first interactive president. The disinformation distributed during the 2020 presidential election contributed mightily to the chaos that our country may have to deal with for a very long time.

In 2010, Facebook's fans rallied to demand that Betty White (at the time eighty-eight and destined to live to ninety-nine) be named to host *Saturday Night Live*. The NBC network agreed, and Ms. White hosted *Saturday Night Live* on May 8, 2010 (the night before Mother's Day) and was quite hilarious.

Many of us regularly use social networking to reconnect with people we've not seen in years, including former contacts, clients, and colleagues. Some people take a proactive approach, using social networking sites to continue uninterrupted a relationship with a coworker after moving to a new company.

Social networking also promotes the creation of affinity groups that bring together people who share certain interests. For many business-people, the great value of such groups is that they allow you to monitor what others are saying about a given topic. I currently belong to twenty-seven different affinity groups, including PwC Alumni, Korn/Ferry Alumni, Hardaway High School Alumni, Columbus State University, Leadership Atlanta, Leadership Georgia, Atlanta CEO Council, Outstanding Atlanta and TEDxAtlanta, to name a few.

A Community Conversation

Two of the most important characteristics of a powerful network are longevity and depth. Staying in contact or reengaging prior relation-ships will help you build a network with which you can interact when the need arises. Try to remember that social networking is about com-munity. It is meant to be a conversation among people or companies, not a one-way means of cramming information down the throat of your target audience. Monologues will not create a long-lasting net-work, whether through traditional networking or social-media network-ing. Conversations, however, can go on a very long time.

How long? Today, according to the Statistic Brain Research Institute, 1 in 5 relationships and a little more than 1 in 6 marriages begin online.

When I wrote the first edition of *Heart of Networking* in 2004, social networking was in its infancy, but it was I who came to it kicking and screaming. I have been a networker all my life, and I love being around people and interacting with them. I didn't simply trash social network-ing in the earlier edition even though I never believed it would amount to much was because I did not want to be on the wrong end of trend as I had when first buying a computer. Luckily, I gambled well because if I *had* trashed it, I'd have come across as no smarter than the flat-Earth folk.

While there are major psychological and practical differences between them, social networking is more like traditional networking than it is different from it. In the end, the digital version gives you much more access to other people, and in return, they have access to you. The distinction is one of volume, not quality. Networking requires *work,* regardless of whether you do it online or in real life.

What I now see about social networking that I missed a half-dozen years ago is the profound value of accessibility. In the flesh, I'm still an incredibly social person. I go to more events than most folks do, and I network when I'm at them. Nevertheless, there is a lag time between the best events in town, and no one can be physically in the loop all the time. Because of the Covid-19 pandemic, my day-to-day, face-to-face networking ended on Friday, March 13, 2020. It was on January 20, 2020, when the Center for Disease Control announced the first U.S. laboratory-confirmed case of Covid-19 in the U.S. from samples taken on January 18 in Washington state. The first two months, it did not really become a thing for most folks. However, in mid-March of 2020, it got serious and although I have had both shots and the booster, I still take this very seriously as I typed this page on July 25, 2022, because as safe as my family has been for two and a half years by wearing one or two masks everywhere, picking up most of our needs from groceries to fast food in the parking lot rather than inside, and not eating inside a restaurant, my wife, daughter, son-in-law and three grandchildren all were infected with Covid-19 in May 2022. I don't want or need to take any unnecessary chances. Period.

Many of us still favor Skype, Zoom, Teams, and other live communication media. I know that even after the all-clear is finally sounded, remote conferencing will continue to be in vogue. This mode of meeting and communicating will continue to be crucial for anyone who wants to be relevant in any field from business to social justice to issues of faith and to keep up with family, friends and clients across the country and the world.

Creating a Presence

Today, you can spread your message and influence across many platforms and reach millions of people. Social networking is traditional networking leveraged spectacularly, and if you are going to be in the game of connecting with people, you must have a presence.

A presence. This doesn't mean that you get online and start talking to people. To create an effective presence, to be successful networking with social media, means creating conversations, not talking, not lecturing, not selling. Converse with people just as you would at any real-life networking event. The best conversationalists spend most of their time listening. Do so online. Listen and learn from the experience of others.

Business is all about trading value for value. The only way you're going to know what other people value is to listen and learn. Education is one of the great benefits of social networking. Many of the best bloggers and Twitter gurus are not talking about themselves or their companies. They are sharing information that might be difficult or impossible to find in any other forum. Every day I follow one or two links that I find in someone's post and discover information I would never have found on my own.

In social media, brevity is gold. I admit that too many of my posts do not reflect my embrace of this rule of thumb. Often, my passion for changing the world gets the best of me, but I continue to work on my aspiration to brevity because I know that no one has the time to read everything I want to share. The best posters provide an idea or a snapshot of a subject and then add a link to the full article, blog, or website. Hyperlinking is the sovereign driver of Internet information. It lets you snap from the big picture into the deeper dive whenever and wherever you want. It allows you to interact with the data, to get what you need when you need it. I cannot count the times that something I learned on the Net was instrumental in creating a new relationship. I have used the knowledge to create conversations at live networking events and to spice up a voicemail left for a prospect. I find that leading with information that immediately and directly helps the other person in their business or their life makes it far more likely that my call will be returned. If you don't promise value, if you use social media only to promote yourself and your business or to sell products, you will soon find yourself on a lot of people's blocked lists and likely be defriended across large swaths of the social network.

"What Can I Do for You?"

As author and entrepreneur Gary Vaynerchuk puts it, the best posting on any social media site is "What can I do for you?" That is the question tailormade to social media, and you can go with it. But I suggest making a slight tweak: *What* may *I do for you?* The "may" implies that doing something "for you" is a pleasure and privilege "for me." That's why savvy salespeople working the salesfloor ask "How may I help you?" rather than "How can I help you?"

Of course, the best opener on a social media post is more targeted and specific—but still interactively questioning: "What is *your* worst experience with IT staffing companies?" Or: "Share with me *your* most appreciated customer service experience." Not "*I* want to sell you *our* IT staffing services."

Ask what you can or may do for the other person, and you will be amazed at the number of responses and conversations that follow. Not only will you find the information you receive extremely helpful, but you will also multiply your social media cred by demonstrating that you get it: *Social media is about conversations, not about riding a one-way street to self-promotion.*

Successful bloggers, Twitter pros, and LinkedIn gurus are followed more often than other people online because their postings are never a closed-ended sales pitch. They are always an open invitation to dialogue. Don't get me wrong, there is time and opportunity to sell yourself, your product, and your company using social media, but it's not the place to begin, and if direct marketing is your only objective, you will find that all your postings generate is radio silence.

6

■

Please Borrow My
Social Networking Toolkit

I AM NOT GOING TO ATTEMPT TO WRITE A DETAILED analysis of every social networking tool available. For one thing, the technology moves like a school of fish, and it's impossible to track what's going to be important and relevant when this book is published, let alone six months after it's in your hands. Social networking sites are as numerous as the stars, and some are almost as far away—from being useful. While they all have value, I'm not equipped to decide what will be the best tool four months from now when this book is published, much less a few years from now when people are just picking up this book to read for the first time. Today, my go-to work sites are LinkedIn, Twitter, and Facebook, in that order. I occasionally visit Pinterest, Instagram, and Snapchat, but I have yet to figure out how to use them for business purposes. However, I find articles where folks say they use these platforms for business, so I will leave it at that, except to suggest that you search "Top 10 Social Media Channels for Business Application."

What I want to share with you is my personal experience with the social networking tools I've found indispensable. Why these? Because I think you will not want to be without them.

Many years ago, I got a call from a good friend, Cindy Tierney, who at that time was the CIO at Beazer Homes. I think very highly of Cindy, and we would be friends regardless of any business connection. She called that day with a dilemma that had nothing to do with business. I tell every client and friend that I do not want to be just their staffing service provider. I want to be their concierge for anything and everything they may need—as long as it is legal, ethical, and moral. (And, yes, I have been asked to do a thing or two over the years that do not meet one or more of the above.) If you become the go-to person whenever someone has a problem, you will create relationships that last a lifetime, a lifetime inside business and out.

The problem Cindy presented to me was her desire to have her daughter Reece's birthday at what was then the soon-to-be-opened Georgia Aquarium in downtown Atlanta. The aquarium's website already announced its birthday party offering, but when my friend called—and called more than a few times—she was told, on each occasion by a different person, that the aquarium had not yet put together the birthday package or determine the costs involved. There was nothing they could do for her, they said, but sell her general-admission tickets, admit her group to the aquarium, and then put them in the snack bar, where they could pull together a few vacant tables (if they could find them!) and have something resembling a party.

Disheartened, she gave me a call. I make it a point to tell every friend, prospect, or client that I am available to them for *any* reason, business or otherwise. It might be about tickets to a concert, a ball game, or, in this case, setting up a birthday party at the Georgia Aquarium. I am not always able to work miracles, but I commit myself to trying to make it happen. That is the value I can realistically offer. So, naturally, I agreed to help in any way that I could.

After hanging up, I racked my brain to discover whom I could call for help. I considered phoning my long-time friend, the late Spurgeon Richardson, who was at the time CEO of the Atlanta Convention and Visitors Bureau and who knew everyone. He would certainly make a call to the aquarium on my behalf. But before calling for that favor, I did a LinkedIn search for names of aquarium employees. Who should pop up on this list but a long-time friend who had left his VP of sales role at a large convention hotel in Atlanta to take the equivalent position at the aquarium! Although I had been out of the hospitality industry for more than fourteen years at the time, I knew he would take my call.

Within hours, I was working with the catering manager to create the first-ever birthday party at the Georgia Aquarium. It was a celebration for fourteen friends in a ballroom that could easily accommodate five hundred people. A long table was placed in front of the floor-to-ceiling window showcasing the Beluga whales. I could not attend the event myself but, based on the thank you card I received from daughter and mother, it had been, quite literally, a once-in-a-lifetime experience. Apart from the satisfaction I receive from giving people an experience they will always remember—and how many times can we do *that?*—I learned a profound lesson about how a relationship created twenty-five years earlier was still meaningful, still capable of paying dividends. All I had to do was reactivate it by reconnecting through social media research.

Another equally effective use of social media happened a few years later. I was scheduled to have lunch with a mid-level executive at a company whose name is known across the universe. A few days before the meeting, I began my due diligence. Based on their level of seniority, I did not think this person would be on Facebook. So, I dug into LinkedIn but could not find a profile. I googled him and, other than a few mentions of his sitting on a panel or making a speech somewhere, found no details that would help further our conversation. I then called a few folks at the company and asked if they knew this person. Turned out, everyone knew him, and they all said he was a great guy and we would hit it off well. When I followed up with a few questions (Is he married? Does he have children? Where did he go to college?), they had no idea. I questioned to myself whether they truly had a relationship with him other than knowing his name and seeing him around the office.

It was the night before the lunch, and out of desperation, I visited Facebook and entered his name. There he was, along with photos of his wife, daughter, and an avalanche of fantastic information. He was even kind enough to list his ten favorite songs, which I downloaded onto iTunes and burned to a CD. The next day, I picked him up at his office and we headed to lunch. I casually slipped in my new CD and watched his ears perk up. At some point, he said that I had a great taste in music, and I replied, "Oh, do you like this as well"?

Needless to say, our lunch went very well. We talked about family, the first time his daughter saw snow, and, of course, music. I would like to point out that he should have known something was up because in my suit, tie, and executive automobile, I hardly embodied the Beastie Boys, Bone Thugs-N-Harmony, or Violent Femmes demographic.

We mostly skipped any discussion of business because my goal was to create a relationship, not make a sale. On our way back to the office, I knew I had to come clean, so, before I parked in front of his office, I told him that I was very glad he enjoyed the music but that I already knew that he would. "I downloaded the ten favorite songs from your Facebook page last night. Why don't you take the CD? These are artists more for your generation than mine."

He looked at me intently, shook his head a few times and said: "You are good, very good."

I graciously accepted his compliment, but, in reality, I was not especially "good." I did nothing that I thought was out of the ordinary. I just took information he had freely shared and leveraged it into a personal moment that changed the meal from a business lunch to a time of fellowship and communion.

It has often been said, "What goes around comes around." The phrase is usually used in the negative, to express the hope that someone will receive their "just" punishment for an act against us or a friend. Time and again, I've been given proof that the axiom works the very same way in the positive direction. Could I ever again pull off something like the special lunch at the aquarium or have a chance to leverage a musical moment into a friendship? Maybe not, but it won't stop me from trying. One thing's for sure, social networking played a key role in making it happen.

LinkedIn

LinkedIn is by far the most popular business social networking tool in the United States. In 2010, when I wrote the second edition of this book, there were some sixty million profiles on LinkedIn. Twelve years later, there are over 800 million users in 200 countries. Sorry I did not own any of this stock.

I use LinkedIn every day. Again, when the second edition was written, I had 1,200 connections. Today, I have close to 8,400 first-degree connections. Do I know every single one of them personally? Of course not. On another note, I turn down at least twenty-five requests from LinkedIn every single day, because I don't want meaningless connections with hordes of people I've never met. I know that when I connect with someone on LinkedIn, they will have access to my life and my business relationships. So, if I don't know you, don't know someone connected to you, or you are not with a company that interests me, I will probably not accept your invitation. It's fair to assume that since we have nothing in common, your intention is to use my contacts or my reputation without first creating a relationship with me. Ease of accessibility should not become a portal to indiscriminate relationships.

In the early 1990s, anthropologist Robin Dunbar theorized that our neocortical processing capacity limits us to knowing in some intimate way only about 150 people. This maximum capacity is called "Dunbar's Number," and it means that we don't have enough brain space to maintain anything like a close relationship with eight thousand fellow beings. Okay, I surrender to Dunbar's Number—but, nevertheless, I *do* know personally and have shared a meal or a phone call with an above-average number of my LinkedIn connections.

In fact, I am not inclined to abandon in the social networking arena the kinds of criteria and standards I live by in my face-to-face networking. In real life, I wouldn't recommend someone to my contacts unless I knew them, understood their value proposition, knew who they do business with, and did business with them in the past. If the past relationship ended, how it ended is also an important consideration. What I would not do in a traditional networking context, I will not do on the web. My reputation and relationships are precious to me, and I treat them with respect in every engagement, regardless of the medium.

As for practical usefulness, I cannot tell you how many times I have used LinkedIn to secure an appointment with just the right person. The ability to find everyone in Atlanta or anywhere else on the planet is invaluable. LinkedIn allows me to learn a great deal about most of my prospects, and it gives me the ability to find everyone who works for the company who also has a LinkedIn profile. In addition, the site enables me to ask one of my personal connections to introduce me electronically to one of their connections. Many times, this digitally empowered version of six degrees of separation has made my day when I'm trying to meet someone new. And, of course, knowing personal information, such as a connection being a University of Georgia or Georgia Tech graduate, opens up great conversations when a meeting is secured. There are "free" versions of LinkedIn and an upgraded version for about $300.00 annually. I pony up $600.00 per year to subscribe to one of LinkedIn's premier services, which gives me access to more people in a given company and more information about people who visit my LinkedIn profile. It also tells me who looks at my profile be it competitor or potential client.

I could fill two books with examples of how LinkedIn has created real business because I knew information that I would not have known without the platform. It is business-focused, so there will be very little personal information like wife, children, or sports played in the past. However, if you know how to dig, there is a wealth of information at your fingertips.

Let me offer just one example of the power of the information available on LinkedIn. When I was the chief development officer at Definition 6, we competed with three other interactive agencies in pitching a large project for a casino in Mississippi. In preparation for the pitch, I researched each person we would be meeting with at the casino, and I discovered through LinkedIn that the general manager had formerly worked at two Ritz Carlton hotels. Having been in the hospitality industry earlier in my career and having owned and operated a transportation company that served both of Atlanta's Ritz Carltons, I knew a lot of the hotel chain's executives. My first email went to Mr. Horst Schultz, former CEO and the driving force behind the international expansion of the chain. Horst kindly responded with everything he knew about his former GM. I then reached out to two other senior Ritz Carlton executives to broaden my picture of our prospect.

Early Sunday afternoon, four of our Definition 6 team members rendezvoused with our founder and truly one of the greatest marketing minds I know, Mr. Michael Kogon, for a long drive to Pearl,

Mississippi, where the two casinos were located. We honed our presentation throughout the entire drive. We were the third of four presenters up to bat the next day. We practiced our presentation for the umpteenth time all morning. You can never overemphasize the value of being prepared.

I started our presentation by thanking the committee for their time. I then looked at the general manager and told him that I had recently corresponded with his old friend, Horst Schultz. He was amazed that I even knew Horst. As for the presentation itself, it went great. Michael Kogon, Chris Thornton, and T. J. Hargen of our team were at the top of their game, so that our creative ideas resonated with everyone in the room. At the close, we asked the committee if they had any questions or wanted us to expand on anything we presented. The GM started his critique with the following words paraphrased from the 1996 movie *Jerry McGuire*: "You had me at *Horst*."

After some other questions, we were told that a decision would be made by Friday, a long four days away. We begin the drive back to Atlanta critiquing our presentation. We all were satisfied that we had done a great job and had met our own personal expectations. As they say in sports. "We left everything on the field." Nevertheless, we did not relish suffering through four nerve-wracking days.

As we approached Anniston, Alabama, my cell rang. It was the GM. He said that they had seen the last presentation, and, after a brief discussion, the decision had been made. There was no reason to wait until Friday. Definition 6 was the right company to be their partner.

Do I believe that my LinkedIn research and the behind-the-scenes networking with Ritz Carlton executives won the business? Of course not. Our presentation was flawless, and the ideas generated by the brilliant creative staff at Definition 6 were the value the selection committee bought. But did my effort help? Without a doubt.

Twitter

Twitter started slowly for me, but I now use it almost as much as LinkedIn and more than Facebook. It is the most effortless platform for sharing information. So far, however, I have received much more from Twitter than I have contributed. That just makes me one of the crowd, because, according to a recent study, 90 percent of community members are lurkers, who read or observe but don't contribute; 9 percent edit or respond to content but don't create content of their own; and just 1 percent create new content.

I am thankful for that 1% who are willing to share, so that we can stay informed about the latest in news, both business and personal.

Twitter is a social networking site that allows users to broadcast brief chunks of information and publish them either to an RSS feed, email, or a number of applications. It's extremely easy to use, and it doesn't require any real commitment on the part of the publisher. It's also a free service, which has received a great deal of well-deserved publicity. Again, for comparison, when I wrote the second edition in 2010, Twitter had 105,000,000 users. Today, that number is 395,000,000 and continues to grow exponentially. I like Twitter especially because it allows rapid-fire updates and because everyone is limited to 280 (up from the original 140) characters per Tweet, so that we are all forced to be concise and to the point: 280 characters is just shy of 60 English-language words, which average 4.7 characters. For a naturally chatty guy like me, this presents a challenge—but a welcome one.

I use Twitter to share positive information about my clients, prospects, and friends. I occasionally post political commentary, which I fear may create more darkness rather than more light. (I am currently working on that.) I have also found Twitter to be invaluable when dealing with personal and business service providers on customer service issues. My all-time favorite "Twitter Miracle" story was when I was having major issues with a cable service provider. I called, cursed, screamed, and probably acted like a three-year-old numerous times on their customer service phone line. With each call I ended up more frustrated. I discovered that they had a regular corporate Twitter Account and a Customer Service Twitter Account, so I created a tweet saying how disappointed I was with their service. Within an hour, I received a direct message from their "Cares Team" asking what they could do for me. The agent went to work, and my problem was solved in less than three hours—*after* I had been told earlier by the phone agent that it would take two days. When I asked the "Cares Agent" how she could do in hours what the local office could not do in days, she told me that she had been given resources the local office did not have.

Very interesting. To me, this suggests something of a new normal for service-focused companies *and* for those customers who know how to use social networking to reach them more effectively. That company is hardly alone in using Twitter to monitor its presence on the Internet. Corporate use of Twitter continues to grow daily.

The great trick to using Twitter effectively is to avoid being boring. It's important to make at least some of your conversations relevant to something other than yourself or your business. If you're connected to a large number of businesspeople, the content stream starts feeling generic, as everyone writes about their jobs. Unless you are a fighter pilot or Volodymyr Zelenskyy, your job probably isn't worth reading about thirty times a day. Just because you can update every thought in your head doesn't mean you should. Make it personal. Make it special. Talk about your family, your coworkers, your charitable work, and the not-for-profit organizations your company supports. Make it real, and you will create real relationships.

There's more that I like about Twitter. There's the ability it gives you to find detailed information on a variety of subjects. Most great Twitter posters include a URL link to their original source. The 280-character tweet allows you to know what the message is about and then gives you the option to take a deeper dive. The heavy use of hash tags has also made it easier to gather information that is important to you. When I attend an event where great information is being shared, I will use the hash tag when I sent tweets highlighting my favorite takeaways. I can't estimate the number of times folks have thanked me for sharing the information from events they had not been able to attend in person.

Another Twitter benefit is the ease with which your tweets can be passed along to a larger population. If you are providing useful information, people in your network will retweet your original posting, sending it to every one of their followers, some of whom will also retweet your content. If there is a better branding tool available, I am not aware of it. When you get second and third parties forwarding your thoughts and insights, you will be amazed at the benefits. New people will begin following you, thereby giving you a larger and larger platform from which to share your passions. In the end, if your leading passion is to educate your audience and create a conversation, you will become one of the most respected and most followed people using social networking, and you will find yourself with a personal brand that is widely respected.

In his brilliant book, *Love Is the Killer App,* motivational speaker and former Yahoo executive Tim Sanders says that "our goal is not to make our prospects, clients, or friends think they are smart. Make them smart!" And that can occur only if you are filling your mind by following the news, reading your industry's publications, and subscribing to the social media platforms and blogs of industry experts.

7

■

Putting Your Brand Online

TRADITIONALLY, WHEN WE THINK OF BRANDING, WE THINK of consumer goods companies like the Coca-Cola Company, Delta Air Lines, or Amazon. Today, however, every one of us is the CEO of Brand Me. We all have a brand that our friends, neighbors, clients, and prospects see when we are together or they are online. Just as big companies have traditionally developed brands to give their products a personality and identity in the minds and hearts of consumers, now individuals are using social media to brand the product that is *them*. There must be a hundred good books on this subject easily found on Amazon. An old one that I have enjoyed and used is *Why Now Is the Time to Crush It* by Gary Vannerchuk, a person I respect for his knowledge but do not enjoy hearing his presentations because of his aggressive usage of foul language, which does not add to his credibility, but rather detracts from it, in my opinion. It is not that I don't know all the four-letter words ever created (and have used them on more than one occasion), I just don't think they add any value. They do offend more people than you may think, and it makes me uncomfortable if others are offended or uncomfortable.

Personally, I try my best to convey the same message of who I am, whether I am with someone face to face, on the telephone, or via social media. As I mentioned, I use LinkedIn, Facebook, and Twitter every day—some days for a few minutes and some days for several hours. I keep all the sites open on my desktop, in addition to Spotify and iTunes. I want a consistent message about myself going out to the public, so I post the same message on all social media sites, because I know that each site appeals to a slightly different audience.

Perhaps you do the same—at least if you are already sold on the idea of personal branding. If you aren't, let me assure you that it is an effective tool to help distinguish you from everyone else in your field. What has long worked for corporate businesses now works for people. Marketers call it "relevant differentiation."

I'm employed by Talent 360 Solutions, a wonderful boutique staffing firm, which provides IT/Engineering/Technology as well as Accounting/Finance talent to Fortune 500 companies and local startups. In almost every sales presentation I make, I say something like "Talent 360 Solutions is unique and different just like the other 300 staffing firms in Atlanta claim to be."

The line always gets a grin of agreement. Staffing is an industry with a lot of competition and a low barrier to entry, but I've really thought about it and could list a dozen attributes of Talent 360 that give us a distinct advantage. I could also tell you a dozen attributes of my own way of doing business that have given *me* an advantage in the marketplace. In both cases, the particulars I could list constitute a brand. The one that I believe is unique to me personally and that I have never heard anyone else in the staffing industry pitch is this: "My passion is to create more new revenue for you than our company receives in revenue for our placements."

Who else offers that? And who else delivers that on a regular basis?

Going the Second Mile

I have nurtured my personal brand for more than four decades. It has allowed me to build strong networks in many different industries as well in in both the business association and civic not-for-profit worlds. Every job I've landed and many of my biggest sales have come through my network. "Your net worth is equal to your network." I'm not sure where I first encountered that formula, but I am convinced that nothing could be truer. In this Internet-driven interactive society, if you do not have a powerful network, your net worth will suffer. Sure, you can find examples of people who made it all on their own. But try stacking up the total net worth represented by that group against the net worth of those who networked. At the very least, I'd venture a financial difference times one hundred.

Networking, however you do it, is work. If you are willing to roll up your sleeves, you are going to be a successful networker.

"There is no traffic jam in the second mile" is another of my favorite sayings. Its origin is Matthew 5:41. Jesus was teaching His disciples how to become exceptional. Back then, a Roman soldier could force any Jew to carry his heavy pack for up to a mile. This casual slavery caused great consternation among the people. In his Sermon on the Mount, Jesus told his disciples, "If someone forces you to go one mile, go two."

Although we face heavy traffic all the time in our personal and professional lives, we can get out of the jams by going a second mile for a client, friend, or loved one, and perhaps cheerfully add a third and a fourth mile when needed. The willingness to do as much will separate you from 99 percent of all the other people in the world. In life as in business, we must remember that our sincere goal should be to help one another. Tom Peters, one of America's most prolific management authors, advised: "Be distinct, or be extinct." Going that second mile will make you distinct and give you the advantage over those who are just too busy being too busy.

My Brand on Facebook

Facebook was originally designed for college students. Early on, in fact, the only way to access Facebook was via your academic institution's email address. Back in the early days of Facebook, I found this infuriating because I couldn't log on.

Facebook was more selective than Myspace or the few other social media networking sites of the mid-2000s because it wasn't open to every schoolchild (or predator) on the block. Basically, Facebook was what happened when the first generation of Myspace users were outgrowing the site. Facebook advertisements were subtle and targeted very specifically, and the interface was designed for relatively sophisticated computer users, who were given a lot of room to customize content. Because early feedback came from users with strong interface preferences, the format was soon streamlined and admirably well organized.

Once Facebook became well established, it was opened to the general population but nevertheless has managed to maintain a level of sophistication Myspace lacked. Once again, for comparison, on June 2010 Facebook had over 400 million users, including me. Four hundred million sure sounds like plenty until you learn that today, July 1, 2022, Facebook has 2.936 billion, 1.9 billion of whom log in every single day. Sixty-five percent of every Facebook user logging in is the main reason that no one wants to be banned from the platform. This is also why Facebook has morphed from a "friends and family" social media site to a huge business platform, which generated $84 billion in advertising revenue in 2020. In 2021, Facebook generated $150 billion in advertising revenue, a $66 billion increase in one calendar year. These are hard numbers to get my brain around, and yet you and I can leverage Facebook every single day without a cash cost to us. Amazing, in my opinion.

A big part of my brand as the go-to person for my key contacts is my absolute willingness to go the second mile, and I use Facebook every day to find information that will help me make the journey. Before social networking, I had to spend hours, days, months, and many meetings getting to know personal information about potential clients. When people were apt to remain business-focused, I would solicit help from their assistants, friends, the doorman, or anyone else I thought could further my quest to understand my clients better.

These days, I have reached a point in my career that many people are sufficiently kind and trusting to volunteer to me more information about their lives than their mother knows about them. But that hasn't always been true. It's taken time.

I have a Facebook page, which gets visited often, and I also have a Facebook "Fan" page for my book and public speaking. I include personal information and pictures that you would not necessarily see at first glance if, for example, you visited my house. My wife and I have frequently discussed whether this level of openness is appropriate. In fact, she would prefer that I had a business Facebook account, which kept private everything about me or my family. I understand her inclination toward privacy, but if I want others to share their information with me, I must trust that I can share mine with them. My brand, after all, is *me*. So, the site becomes personal: pictures from vacations, family gatherings, and every celebrity I have been fortunate to meet are all grouped together for the world to see. My belief is that people are drawn to candor. I do not hide my personal beliefs concerning faith, community service, politics, or any other potentially controversial subject. Couldn't hide these things even if I wanted to. In the era of a twenty-four-hour news cycle, people have learned to spot a phony in about two seconds flat. Want to have positive impact?

You must be real.

I had never really focused on being "real" because I have always tried to just be me. I don't put on airs and because I don't feel or believe I am superior to anyone. When I receive greater than normal praise or recognition for something I did for someone else or the community, I have a great deal of angst accepting it. Rather than be humble and gracious, I often try to make a joke out of it or use a reference that would quickly deflate the praise. I know that is not how I should handle it and I am sure I have offended a few folks who were just being kind. That is on me. While I was a Director over Business Development for emerging growth companies within Pricewaterhouse Coopers, I had the privilege of working with the most wonderful human being, Mrs. Susan O'Dwyer. Susan ran marketing for our area, and she did not suffer fools lightly and on more than one occasion, she had to put me in my place for getting too far out of my lane. I appreciated her passion and guts to stand face to face with someone twice her size and say no. We developed an amazing relationship and I consider her one of the special people in my life.

For instance, in December of 1999, I was hired by Pricewaterhouse-Coopers in their Audit & Tax division focused on emerging growth technology companies. I may have been the only person ever hired by the biggest of what was then the Big 5 accounting firms, who did not know the difference between a debit and a credit. What my boss (and soon dear friend) Dan Giannini saw in me was my passion to make connections. At that time, of the Big 5 in the emerging technology space, PwC was a distant sixth or seventh place. With Dan's leadership and the marketing expertise of Susan O'Dwyer, an incredible woman who had an uncanny ability to help me focus, we owned—within a single year—the emerging growth space in Atlanta for accounting firms.

I would love to write a few chapters on how we accomplished this, but, at its heart, it was simple: we broke all the rules and decided to be real, putting humanity and fun into an accounting world that was fairly stodgy at the time. Susan was in charge of making sure all I promised came true and then cleaning up the wreckage of what happens when a tornado goes through a town. I don't remember if Susan told me this while we were working together or after I left for Korn/Ferry, but nonetheless hear the story from Susan directly:

Working with Ricky Steele was an adventure in laughter, humility and love. No two days were ever the same—which is saying something at a staid accounting firm! — except for the fundamentals of decency and dignity with which Ricky accorded everyone he encountered. Ricky's sense of humor is second to none and it made him irresistible to all, from CEOs to the clerks behind the Krispy Kreme counter. At the heights of the dot.com boom in 2000, there was no lack of ego in tech startup founders. They all, however, sought out Ricky, who never once wavered in how he treated everyone—with a joke to start, an answer or referral to someone with the answer, a thoughtful commitment to make helpful introductions and connections, but always, also, a caring heart for that person as a person, not just as a "source of revenue" to our employer, the accounting firm.

Not a week went by that I didn't receive a phone call or get stopped at a meeting from those same CEOs who all wanted to know the same thing. "Is he for real?" They just couldn't get over that, all in one package, someone could be that that genuinely funny, helpful and caring. I assured each of them that, with Ricky, what they saw and/or heard, was who he actually was.

No guile or ulterior motives. Completely transparent.

I learned more from Ricky about servant leadership, how to really live out my Christian faith, and the irresistible power of a heart for others, than I have in a lifetime of sermons. Yes, he IS the "real deal" and you'd be wise to incorporate his suggestions into making a better you!

I am grateful to Susan for sharing that very kind illustration with me and for allowing me to share it with you.

You must be real if you expect reality from others. There are certainly some personal issues that stay within the family, and I never expose anything negative or hurtful about any other individual. Otherwise, I do share from my heart, and, based on the feedback I receive from my speaking engagements and personal relationships, I share a consistent message.

I am grateful for all the "real" stuff business leaders and others share on Facebook, and that is why I do the same. I don't think I'm alone in wanting to know as much as possible about the lives of those with whom I do business. It is all part our brand—who we are, what we stand for.

Blog Your Brand

At some point, if you are interested in becoming a voice among your colleagues, bosses, and customers, you will want to begin blogging. Blogging is no more than sharing your passion about life, your business, the world, and everything in between.

I have been blogging off and on for over ten years now. I know I should do it more because when I do, I see results. With the unlimited amount of space available for a blog post as opposed to a Twitter post, you can get deeper into messages about what is important to you. So far, my most-read post was a link to a much longer post I made on LinkedIn about the Confederate battle flag issue which I posted shortly after the murder of George Floyd. Between Twitter and LinkedIn, over 77,000 people Liked, Loved, or

Shared the article. That is the most folks who have ever connected with anything I have ever posted by a multiple of 10.

I felt compelled to write the article about what certain folks in politics were saying—that it was acceptable to fly the Confederate battle flag because Southerners loved and respected it so very much. I wrote a long and personal counterpoint article, which argued that it was no more acceptable to fly the Confederate battle flag than it would be to fly a Nazi or Japanese World War II battle flag. Many people would not have broached this controversial and partisan subject because it might cost them customers. I had a few friends tell me precisely that after I published the piece. I appreciated it, but I believed—and do believe—deeply that we all have to be faithful to our truth. If that costs me business, so be it.

I use Word Press.com to publish my blog, but there are many other free platforms. My blog also has an RSS feed, so that my regular readers can subscribe, receiving any new blog I post. There are many books and articles on blogging, and the ones I shared in the 2010 edition of this book are obsolete. The same will be quickly true of any reference I publish now. So, I suggest you just google "Blogging for business" and turn up dozens of fresh articles and books on the subject. I also highly recommend that you subscribe to the podcasts of people in your field, your competitors, and experts in anything that interests you. You can build quite a following by reading, commenting about, and forwarding blogs and podcasts you find helpful.

Public Speaking (a/k/a Blogging, Old School)

Blogging may be a new idea to many of us, but it can be looked at as a new digital take on a very old analog venue: the public speech. Just as online social networking cannot completely replace traditional face-to-face networking, so blogging cannot give you the literally in-your-face presence that a good speech delivers. According to well-documented surveys, many people rate public speaking *ahead* of death as their worst fear, so I understand if you find the prospect of getting up in front of a group daunting. That said, failing to take advantage of this real-life media outlet can hobble a career.

Start by finding a subject you are passionate about and create a presentation around it. After you have built your presentation, take a Dale Carnegie course or join Toastmasters International. This will allow you to practice your speaking skills in front of receptive and supportive audiences, who will coach you along the way. Once you are ready to step beyond the support realm, seek groups with which you can share your knowledge. Every club, civic association, and corporation is on the lookout for subject matter experts. You may even get paid for your speech—or at least snag a free meal (quality not guaranteed). Unless you are Seth Godin, Guy Kawasaki or Mark Cuban, the money will never be as important as the exposure.

I have given my "Heart of Networking" presentation at least five hundred times over the last twenty years, and I never tire of delivering practically the identical speech every time. I am passionate about the subject, and I want to share with new audiences what I have learned over the years. I have also been paid handsomely from time to time, though for every paid speech, I have given twenty-five or thirty First Amendment Speeches. Each of these, in other words, was a Free Speech. I often quip that when I began speaking in public and writing books, I did not do it to make any money. I wanted to share my passion. (So far, my business plan is working perfectly.)

Why do I speak to every church, civic, or corporate group that invites me, even after they tell me there is no budget for a speaker? It is because every presentation gives me a chance to teach my passion, to help others in their job search or in their quest to become more effective at whatever they do. I also do it to get exposure to a new group of people. Most of the first edition of this book was sold at speaking engagements. Gaining exposure has given me new opportunities to publicize my business interests.

In every speech, I share what I do in my regular business, and I tell everyone that I would love to serve them in any way that I can. Ninety-five percent of the people who come up to the podium after I finish are either looking for a job or an introduction to a company they are targeting for sales purposes. I do my best to help each one because I experience great joy in serving others. However, 5 percent of the people who come up become friends for life and, in some cases, clients.

A speaking engagement with the alumni of the Kennesaw State University MBA program created instant success for one of my companies. I gave my usual presentation and mentioned what I do for a living, which lasted less than one minute out of a fifty-minute presentation. The first person to greet me after I finished was Donna Orban, MBA, who at that time was the Manager Strategic Division at Genuine Parts Company, another great Georgia success story and in the Fortune 250. Donna introduced herself, telling me that her company needed a web developer and asking if I might have any interest in working on that position. I immediately asked her if I could wash her car and pick up her dry cleaning, too. I was not interested. I was ecstatic.

What a joy when something happens that is completely unexpected but certainly appreciated. The speech was on a Tuesday morning. The web developer my company found for Donna started the following Monday morning. Since then, Donna introduced me to the vice president of HR for this Fortune 300 company. I am so thankful for the kindness Donna showed me that day. It remains the swiftest meeting-to-success story I have experienced because that placement and introduction created what became my largest client for several years. A "Free Speech" that generates tens of millions in revenue for your company and over $1,000,000 in commissions over years the years is not really a Free Speech. What a blessing!

As I mentioned in talking about John Yates, I was deeply involved some years ago with the United Way of Atlanta's Technology Initiative. I did not chair the initiative but was MC for a series of events that invited CIOs to be on a panel, sharing their focus for the coming year and why they donated time and money to the United Way. This gave me an opportunity to be onstage with four CIOs and in front of an audience of CIOs and other technology folk from across Atlanta.

This was the same panel where I met Bill VanCuren, CIO of NCR, and I want now to tell you more about what happened after I met him. At the end of the presentation and after the attendees departed, I gave as a thank you gift and as an introduction to me personally a copy of an earlier edition of this book to each CIO with a personal inscription. Roughly two months later, I was attending the Inspire Georgia CIO of the Year Awards ceremony. One of the speakers was Bill Nuti, CEO of NCR. So, Bill VanCuren was hosting his boss at the meeting. After Mr. Nuti spoke, I walked up to Bill, whom I had not seen since the United Way panel months earlier. I told him that I thought his boss's presentation was great. He said that he had been meaning to call me to thank me for the book. Bill is from the Midwest and said that my Southern manners and belief system were very similar to his. He then said that he would like to get to know me better by having lunch together. I told him that I was ready. Where do you want to go? He laughed and told me his assistant would email me with some dates in the next few weeks.

I probably don't have to tell you that I did my homework before the meeting. I discovered that Bill VanCuren had two high school sons. I visited their Facebook pages to discover that during the past summer, one worked as a bag boy/delivery person at Kroger and the other at Publix. The lunch was wonderful, and I inquired about his boys, remarking how they worked hard for money over the summer when I knew at his salary level that might not have been necessary.

"Ricky," he said to me, "I have met with a lot of folks over the years, and no one has ever done as much research to create a positive first lunch. I am impressed. Now, tell me a little about your company."

I replied by saying, "We said an hour. Let's do that on our next visit."

"Aren't you in the IT staffing business?"

I answered that I was, and Bill asked if I had any interest in doing business with his company.

"I had not intended to get so deep into business on our get-to-know-you lunch, but of course I would be honored to do business with you and your company."

I will remember that lunch until the day I depart from this earth. A company of his size is normally a month, or two sales cycle followed by another month or two completing paperwork to receive a Master Service Agreement. I left the restaurant on that Friday afternoon to drive to Athens, Georgia, to spend the weekend. I drove back to my office on Monday morning and, before noon, the paperwork to begin the MSA process from NCR arrived by email.

Since that lunch, as I already shared, Bill has become a dear friend, we have done a lot of business with each other, and we work together on two not-for-profit organizations. Did it happen because I was on-stage one morning as the MC of an event? Did it happen because I gave Bill a copy of my book? Or did it happen because I put the "work" into my "Networking"? It doesn't really matter at this point, but if you are doing all you can to create a relationship first before business is generated, there is no end to the possibilities. Really, there no limit to what you can accomplish if you give of yourself by writing and speaking and teaching others how to succeed.

President Jimmy Carter and Ricky Steele at Carter Center reception for Atlanta's Table. Steele was the founder and Chairman of the Board, President Carter was the Honorary Chairman.

President Jimmy Carter and Ricky Steele when Steele was selected to be on the Carter Center Board of Councilors, 35 years after serving together on the Atlanta's Table Board.

Garth Brooks and Ricky Steele at The Ron Clark Academy, 2008

Ludacris and Ricky Steele at the 2017 "Taste of the Nation" Fundraiser for the Atlanta Community Food Bank

Mark Cuban and Ricky Steele at the Jimmy Blanchard Leadership Conference 2014

Seth Godin, Author/Keynote Speaker/Futurist/Marketing Guru and Ricky Steele with Seth's 807-page book, This Might Work *at the Jimmy Blanchard Leadership Conference, 2016*

50+ Friends/Volunteers at the Ann Cramer/Becky Blalock/Bill Bolling/Ricky Steele 3rd Annual Birthday Bash Fundraiser for the Atlanta Community Food Bank

Becky Blalock/Ann Cramer, Ricky Steele and Bill Bolling enjoying our Joint Birthday Party while raising funds for the Atlanta Community Food Bank in 2019

Rob Johnson,/Judge Dorothy Beasley/Bill Bolling/Ricky Steele, the Founders of Atlanta's Table, a division of the Atlanta Community Food Bank, 2016

Ricky Steele, Co-Founder of Atlanta's Table, and Bill Bolling, Founder of the Atlanta Community Food Bank, accepting a check for Atlanta's Table from the Georgia Chapter of MPI in 1987

John Smoltz and Ricky Steele after Ricky threw out the ceremonial "First Pitch" at Turner Field before an Atlanta Braves game on the 10th Anniversary of Atlanta's Table in 1996

Michelle Malone, Beth Steele, Ricky Steele and Trish Land at Michelle's Surprise Birthday Party at Eddie's Attic, 2016

United States Representative, the late Honorable John Lewis, and Ricky Steele at a Lewis campaign event in 2015

Ted Turner aka Captain Courageous and Ricky Steele at the Atlanta Convention and Visitors Bureau Annual Meeting, 2016

Malcolm Gladwell and Ricky Steele at the Jimmy Blanchard Leadership Conference, 2010

William B. Turner, former Chairman of Synovus, TSYS, W.C. Bradley, Board of Directors of The Coca-Cola Company and my mentor for over 50 years and me at the Jimmy Blanchard Leadership Conference 2010

Ricky Steele moderating a panel of CIO's at the United Way Technology Initiative Annual Meeting 2010

Ricky Steele aka "World's Tallest Jockey" with CIO Legendary Leader, the late Mr. Ed Steinike, at the TechBridge Digital Ball 2015

Former United State Senator, the late Max Cleland presenting Ricky Steele with the 1986 Georgia Small Business Person of the Year as recognized by the United States Small Business Administration

Honorable Mayor Andre Dickens, Bill Bolling, Qaadirah Abdur-Rahim and Ricky Steele at the TechBridge Awards Ceremony at The Carter Center 2018

*Michael Dell, Founder of
Dell Corporation, and
Ricky Steele at a VIP
Reception for CIO's at
Dell Secureworks in 2015*

*Ricky Steele, MC and Moderator of a CIO panel discussion, with Bill
VanCuren/NCR, Ed Steinike/The Coca-Cola Company,
Becky Blalock/Southern Company*

*Ricky Steele introducing his mother, Carol Steele, to legendary actor
Burt Reynolds after the World Premier of "Sharkey's Machine"
at the Georgia Governor's Mansion in 1981*

*Ricky Steele, Singer-Songwriter-Actor Loudon Wainwright III and Beth Steele in
Loudon's dressing room after his 2018 City Winery show.*

Jimmy Etheredge, CEO of North America for Accenture, and Ricky Steele in "Booth 61 with Ricky Steele" interview before the Digital Ball 2017

Ricky Steele interviewing Atlanta's technology foundational leader, Mr. John Yates, on "Booth 61 with Ricky Steele" radio show at the CIO of the Year Awards 2017

8
■
Speed Bumps

SO LET'S SAY YOU MANAGE TO WALTZ THROUGH ALL SIX of the degrees that separate you from your target. The fact that you've connected the dots to Mr. Nirvana does not oblige him to agree to a meeting with you anymore than finding someone's home address obliges the home-owner to answer the knock at his door. Taking the trouble to target someone who may well be interested in what you have to offer can be an invaluable ticket to ride, but there is no guarantee you'll ever leave the station.

Meeting the Unmeetable

From time to time, I'll leave a voice message with a person I want to meet, and, in it, drop the name of a venture capitalist or someone else who told me about him. My prospect doesn't always call me back, however. When that happens, I call him again. If I get no response this time, I conclude that he obviously hasn't read my bio and press clip-pings, so he absolutely does not know how lucky he would be to meet me!

Seriously though, what's my next move?

I keep my eye out. When I go to an event and the prospect's name pops out at me as I scan the name badges, I decide right then and there that he *is* going to meet me tonight. Why? I recognize that somebody I know on the list of attendees knows him. How do I know this? I have read and reread my database file on this man.

When I see that common acquaintance walk in, I go up and say, "Bill, I know you know John Smith at the Widget Company, and I have wanted to meet John forever. I don't even know what he looks like. Will you introduce me when he comes in?"

"Of course, I will. He's standing over by the door. Let's go over there now."

When I'm introduced, John remarks, "Oh yes! I've gotten a couple of phone messages from you, and I've been out of town a lot and haven't gotten a chance to return your call."

His next words, as he sees me with Bill, might be an invitation: "Why don't you call me back tomorrow, and let's find time to have lunch. It's just too hard to talk here." Or he might say: "Can you give me an idea what you're calling about?"

Now it's up to me to surprise him. He expects me to say something beginning with the words "I want"—"I want to talk to you about our new line of . . ." or "I want to see if you're in the market for . . ." But that's not how I play it.

"If you could give me fifteen minutes of your time," I say, "I'd like to hear about some of your biggest challenges, because I believe I may have a helpful idea for you. If not, we'll go on our way, both knowing a little bit more about somebody new. Would it be okay if I called your assistant tomorrow morning and set up a time to meet?"

If you make a connection through a mutual friend, then offer a gift instead of asking for something, the response rate will be almost 100 percent positive, which is 100 percent better than an unreturned phone call.

Make Sure the Obstacle Isn't You

Sometimes, it seems, we live on the wrong side of Alice's famous looking glass, a world in which words mean the opposite of what they should mean. Here's an example. You run into somebody you want to network with. He's in a hurry. "Give me a call," he shouts over his shoulder as he trots away from you. Years of through-the-looking-glass conditioning would prompt most of us on the receiving end in this situation to assume that what the guy *really* means is *"Don't* give me a call." And we oblige by never calling him.

That is a mistake. How do you correct it? Don't step through the looking glass.

If someone says to me, "Give me a call," I take that request at face value and the person at her word. Moreover, I will call sooner rather than later, because I want her to know that talking to her is high on my to-do list. Also, I want to make contact before she forgets that she asked me to call. Once it does leave her mind, I've either allowed the opportunity to be greatly diminished or lost altogether. It is one thing to meet with me because *I* asked for it, and quite another to meet because *you* wanted it. In the first instance, I am taking. In the second, I am giving—and I know that I am always in a more powerful position when I have something to give.

Unless the person really is in a hurry, nail down her request immediately.

"Give me a call."

"I can call you tomorrow," I reply, "but if you're going to be busy, I'll call the first of next week."

"I'm going to be out of town until the first of the week. Could you call me next Monday, and we'll try to get together at the end of the following week?"

"Absolutely. I will call you next Monday."

And right then and there I make a note—not a mental note, but a written note, either in my smartphone or notebook—complete with name and day. I *will* make the call, and I will make it when we agreed that I would. The result will be a sense of satisfaction in the other person. Everyone is pleased when promises are kept, and things work the way they're supposed to. In my own case, I know that I have no interest in doing business with someone who says he'll give me a call and then waits two weeks to do it. If he's not conscientious enough to call me when he says he will, then I can't trust that he'll follow through on any other piece of business. I always try to do what I say I'm going to do, and I try to be as timely as possible in doing it. That's what I expect from others. Why shouldn't others expect it from me?

Avoiding a Dead End

I don't know what percentage of movies since cinema's earliest days have included somewhere the line, "Do you believe in love at first sight?" but I bet it's well up in the double digits. I'm not going to debate this question here, because I suspect that if you think you've experienced love at first sight, then you believe in it, and if you think you haven't, then you don't. However, I would suggest that it's not a good idea to stake your emotional, spiritual, and physical future on the mere *possibility* of love at first sight. Talk to your married friends, and you'll find that most long-lasting relationships don't start with a spark that makes them seem, from the first instant, inevitable. Most long-lasting relationships are forged over time. In fact, you may find that many of your married friends didn't even particularly like each other when they first met.

Life is not a snapshot. It's a movie, unrolling over time. Nevertheless, there is a risk that your first contact with a potential client or customer will be your last. You cannot stake your future on the hope that this contact will be the business equivalent of love at first sight, that it will inevitably blossom into a long-term commitment. The savvy networker takes steps to ensure that the first contact won't be a dead end.

The fact is that you don't get to know someone the first time you meet him or her—or the second or third time, for that matter. As I mentioned earlier, I've known people for years and still don't feel I *really* know them. These are my acquaintances, and I have many more acquaintances than people I know well.

Getting to know someone requires commitment from both people. I can't know you if you don't allow me to know you. I can't know you if I don't make an investment of time and energy in knowing you. But what motivates such an investment?

If I'm in a group and I see someone I've wanted to meet for a long time and get to know, I look for a mutual friend or business associate to make an introduction.

If I don't know such an intermediary, I walk directly to my prospect and introduce myself: "Hi, I'm Ricky Steele. I've heard so much about you. I have a couple of ideas I'd like to run by you, but"—and I hasten to add this—"this isn't the place to do that. Could I have permission to call your secretary tomorrow and get scheduled in your calendar for a fifteen-minute meeting?"

I've never had anyone turn down my request for a brief meeting when I put it this way and in these circumstances. Had I cornered this guy at this time and place, he might well have resented an ambush, and our first contact would have been our last. Instead, I shaped the first contact so that it remained open-ended, almost begging to be continued, like an unanswered question or the opening chords of a piece of music. I did this by letting him know that I know his time is at a premium, and, by this means, I demonstrated my respect for him. I was also genuinely helpful: I didn't put him on the spot. Moreover, I stroked his ego just a tad by letting him know that I had heard about him from a variety of people. Perhaps most important, I presented myself as a giver rather than a taker; I let him know that *I* have already invested time in trying to talk to him, and I told him that I have information he might find helpful.

This is quite a package to deliver at first contact, and it took me all of sixty seconds to deliver it. It is a spark that stands a good chance of kindling a lasting relationship, but, unlike the hoped-for spark of love at first sight, there is nothing random or accidental about this one. I've thought about it, prepared for it, and I've carefully shaped the moment.

Now, good as it is, this isn't even a particularly compelling example of a productive first contact. If I do my homework diligently enough, I can usually associate some salient fact with my prospect as I approach him. For instance, if my research has revealed something about him that I find remarkable, I communicate that information to him in the first minute.

"I thought it fascinating how you were able to raise $20 million in the Boy Scout campaign last year when no one thought it could possibly go over $10 million."

Having said this, I might have him for the next hour. If the time and place aren't right for an extended conversation, however, I am certainly guaranteed that he'll be anxious to meet with me later.

The Elevator Pitch
Chance encounters happen all the time. Be prepared to take advantage

of them. This means that you *must* have a two- or three-minute "elevator pitch." This phrase—and the thing it describes—became popular in the late 1990s as the venture capital world exploded. Conferences were being held all over the world, with VCs meeting all sorts of companies and individual entrepreneurs who were looking for funding. Many times, entrepreneurs would find themselves on an elevator with a VC they had been trying to meet for months. In this situation, they had about two or three minutes during the ride to make a presentation. If it was not compelling, once the door opened, the VC vanished—forever.

While the universe of venture capital has changed considerably since the go-go nineties, you still need an elevator pitch. It is an appealing verbal package that says who you are, what you represent, what your company's values are, what makes you unique, and why the person next to you should want to spend any time with you. Your prospect has two questions uppermost in mind: What is your background? What gives you the right to ask for my time?

William Faulkner, who won a Nobel Prize for his novels, once remarked that he wrote novels because short stories were too hard to write. Being concise, packing in, and presenting only the most vital and compelling information is a demanding task, far too demanding to be left to the spur of the moment. Write out your elevator pitch, then practice it in front of the mirror at least fifty times. Refine and rework the pitch after each rehearsal, if necessary. (Note: It *will* be necessary.) Then take it on the road, practicing in front of your spouse, children, co-workers, and really good friends. Ask them to be critical. Make more changes.

Now you are ready. The goal of the elevator pitch is not to make a sale but to obtain a more extended, sit-down appointment for a later time. Once your pitch is finished, don't wait for a reaction. Thank the person for taking the time to listen to your ideas and *ask* permission to call his or her assistant to set up an appointment.

"I want to hear more about your company," you say, "so that we can determine if my product is the best solution for you. If it doesn't look like a good fit, I have many contacts, and I'll keep on the lookout for a solution that *will* work."

It is not easy to refuse someone who promises to help whether or not he makes a sale. However, if you do receive a no, reply with polite thanks and go your way. You have prospects who *do* want to see you, and if you spend a great deal of time preparing for a meeting you bullied someone into accepting, your results will rarely repay the cost of the time.

An elevator ride or similar encounter presents an opportunity to strike a spark. It also carries the risk of turning this guy off for good, either with irrelevant conversation or an awkward silence. Whether you prattle on or keep your mouth shut, the executive will conclude that spending three minutes with you in an elevator is a long, long trip. Instead, make the trip productive by delivering a great elevator pitch. Keep it under three minutes. You've probably witnessed someone who is forced to listen to a longer elevator pitch. He's scanning the elevator —or the room—broadcasting a silent message that says: *This guy is driving me crazy! He won't shut up! I was kind enough to ask him what he was selling, and now he won't let me go.* Commit the sin of an overly long elevator pitch, and you'll soon find yourself on the list of people others want to avoid at the next meeting.

Pack into those two or three minutes the facts that will interest the *other person.* Identify the strongest, most relevant selling point of your product in a succinct manner. Here's an example: "I'm with Acme Widget Company. Our widgets are made with water from the East Coast, a process that gives our widgets three times more strength and durability than those made with West Coast water. I've been in the community for more than ten years, and I'm a long-time Nature Conservancy member, just like you. I know that you're the widget-buyer for your company. Could I call your assistant tomorrow morning and make an appointment for fifteen minutes of your time to show you our widgets?"

On the Nature of No

As I just mentioned, it can be a real advantage to get to *no* sooner rather than later—provided that *no* would have been the answer all along and that it really does mean *no*. Sometimes, however, *no* isn't *no*. It may mean, "No, not today." Or it may mean, "I really don't understand what you're trying to sell me."

Analyzing *no* requires a delicate exercise of judgment. If I believe that my contact and I are communicating well enough that I feel there is an unspoken reason behind his no, I won't say thanks and rush to take my leave. Before I give up, I'll first press a little harder to get at the reason for the negative response. Once I have a good idea of what that reason might be, I'll go ahead and provide more information.

But I always know when to stop—for now. If my contact tells me, "No, Ricky, we've already picked someone else," then I'll smile and reply, "If I ever have anything that fits another niche, can I call you?" No one's ever said no to that, and so I've accomplished two important things. I've identified or retained a potential customer for the future, and I've transformed a meeting that threatened to end negatively into a meeting that ended with a yes. The fact that I didn't make a sale today is far less important than that.

9

■

Networking as Investing

So far, we've covered what I consider the basic principles of effective networking, and we've looked at approaches to making the kinds of contacts that spark the creation of networks. Now I suggest we slice into the subject from a slightly different angle.

Too many people think of networking as a kind of adjunct to business, something that certainly can make doing business easier and more profitable, perhaps, but not something that is *absolutely* necessary.

They are mistaken.

If you believe as I do, that at the heart of business is an exchange of value for value, then networking goes to the very heart of business. Look at it this way: Business requires investment. The seller invests in his product so that he can find a buyer to invest in that product. Both parties must bring value to the transaction. If the seller fails to bring value, his product is valueless and, therefore, will not find a buyer. If a buyer fails to bring value, he cannot legitimately purchase the product. Like any product a business produces, networking requires an equitable exchange of value for value. Like any product a business produces, networking requires investments from both the seller and the buyer.

Information, Please

Before either seller or buyer can invest, they both need information. As I mentioned earlier, when I meet someone for the first time, my goal is to find out enough to fill several note cards with information. Much as I want the information for my database, I am interested first and foremost in the life of the other person. You can't gather the information you need if you approach it as a kind of surveying task. You must enter into a genuine conversation motivated by genuine interest. If you try to fake this, you will be found out, and your opportunity to create a connection will be lost. Body language is a powerful communicator of sincerity, and eye contact is critical.

Often, even before I approach my prospect, I address questions about him or her to someone else at an event, especially if I noticed the two chatting together earlier in the evening. Of course, I only speak to an intermediate person I know fairly well, because I don't want the Stalker Police to drag me out of the event before the night is over. Once I make contact, I work overtime to maintain and build the relationship. I look for new information about my prospect every time I meet him or talk with one of his acquaintances.

After the first meeting, I try to send an e-mail telling my new contact how much I enjoyed making his or her acquaintance. I try to mention something personal we may have shared. For instance, a new contact mentioned that he and his wife are huge Georgia Bulldog fans, having graduated from Georgia in 1975 and 1976, respectively. At the event, I resisted the urge to get on my all fours and holler, "Hunker down, you hairy Dogs," although I have come close to doing this very thing on more than one occasion. But I did file away the information, and I'll be sure to mention it in my follow-up e-mail. Someday, too, I know that I am going to get a call or hear of someone having four tickets to see the Southeastern Conference Championship Game, which after winning the College Football National Championship this past 2021 season, Georgia is destined to play in the SEC Conference Championship for many years to come. When the tickets come my way, I'll buy them, then call my contact, inviting him and his wife to the game. Or, better yet, I may just give them the tickets and let them decide who to take with them. This is a sacrifice for me, but it can produce only one reaction: "What a guy! He could have taken me to the game, and I would have been obligated to listen to his pitch both on the way to the game and back again. But no. I can see he is truly interested in building a relationship. That is the kind of person I want to get to know." If I avoid trying to sell something, I can go a long way toward establishing a valued friend, who, when the time is right, will find it very easy and very natural to do business with me.

Work It

Networking is work, pure and simple, and you cannot become a successful networker until you accept that fact. I am always amazed when I hear someone say that he's not afraid of hard work. I surmise that he has probably never really done any. Most everyone is aware that hard work never killed anybody but regardless they are just not willing to take the chance.

Seriously, a successful networker is busy making calls, attending events, going to meetings, and when he's not doing these things, he's busy doing his homework and becoming a more and more efficient sponge for information. Every article you read about a company or individual gives you additional insight. Read, read, read, then cut, cut, cut, paste, paste, paste. Keep your databases up to date. Train your assistant, if you are fortunate to have one these days, to be as aware of your clients and prospects as you are. Your assistant will be an extra set of eyes and ears, alert to information wherever it may be found.

Sources of information are everywhere. As mentioned earlier, you should do Internet searches for everyone on your need-to-meet list. Google knows more about you than even you know about yourself. There are many other powerful search engines, not to mention LinkedIn and even Facebook, that are valuable resources. Be sure to search not only for his or her formal name, but also for nicknames.

Search for records or articles about the person's company, and don't forget to search for any of the company's current clients. Don't be afraid to pay for information on potential clients through services offered by companies such as Equifax and Hoovers; however, you must draw the line at prying, invading privacy, or doing anything illegal or that even smacks of industrial espionage. Confine your search to what can be found through publicly available sources, including the paid services. Sometimes paid services are helpful and sometimes they are a waste; however, at worst, they are a fairly inexpensive waste, and they may provide just the information needed to help finish piecing the puzzle together.

The more you know about your contact, the greater the odds that you will be able to offer the kind of value he or she wants. Obviously, it is to the advantage of both of you to find out as much as you can before you have an extended meeting. However, it is during the meeting itself that you can learn the most. As I've already mentioned, I make it a practice to arrive a few minutes early to an appointment, so that I can speak to my prospect's receptionist or secretary. Then, once I am ushered into my prospect's office, I take a mental snapshot of the space, looking for evidence of just what interests this person. I don't treat any of this data casually, but, just as I do with conversations and newspaper clippings, I enter my impressions into my database as soon as I get back to my office or home. Sometimes, if something especially interesting catches my eye, I lead the conversation with this item. My assumption is that if whatever I saw is prominent enough to capture my attention, this is what my prospect intended, because the item reflects something of significant interest to him or her. If, as a result of my bringing up the item, this potential client spends thirty minutes telling me about family, hobbies, or passions in life, I may not be able to make my pitch right then and there, let alone write a dime's worth of business. I have, however, made a friend, and that means that there will be additional opportunities to talk business in the future.

Express interest in what interests the other person, but never fake anything. Very few people are fooled by strained insincerity. The key to developing relationships is not what kind of act you put on, but how well you allow other people to see how real you are.

Distinguish Yourself

The purpose of researching your contact is not only to demonstrate that you can serve her needs most effectively, but to separate yourself from the rest of the pack vying for this person's time. Study your prospect so that you can do meaningfully extraordinary things to get her undivided attention. Search your database, your dossier on this contact, for clues to what floats this individual's boat. If it's a college football team, how hard is it to send a clipping when his team has a big upset win over a higher ranked opponent? It may be golf, or tennis, community service, or faith. *Something* in your prospect's life amounts to a passion. Once you become aware of that passion, go out of your way to celebrate it with that person. Then watch him or her build bridges for you.

Networking is a thinking person's foundation for growth and the opportunity to change the community, if not the world. The prize consistently goes to the most creative. I have always tried to go over the top in pleasing my clients or in securing new ones. For instance, I was once given the opportunity to bid on a transportation contract with the McDonald's Corporation for a rather large convention in Atlanta.

I was picking up three meeting planners at the airport and driving them to their headquarters hotel, the Omni. I knew the planners would be running late and that they would not have had time to get lunch before a series of afternoon meetings. I called the VP of marketing at the Omni and, together, we literally cooked up a unique greeting for *his* guests and *my* potential clients. I sent my best chauffeur to the airport in our finest Rolls Royce Phantom V limousine. In another limousine, I dispatched the Omni chef and his assistant to the airport. I met the planners at the gate—a privilege we no longer enjoy in an era of heightened security—and escorted them to the waiting Rolls. Once they were comfortable, I popped open a bottle of Dom Perignon just as the Omni chef and his assistant walked up, clad in immaculate dress whites and tall hats. They were carrying large silver serving platters covered with the big silver sliding hemisphere, the kind of covered platter seen in five-star restaurants.

With a flourish, the chef slid back the cover—to reveal an assortment of McDonald's hamburgers, French fries, and milk shakes. Predictably (to me, anyway), the planners laughed until they cried. They even ate the food on the way to the hotel, although the Omni did have a full meal prepared on their arrival.

Do you think I received the business? Don't doubt it for a minute. And many of the company's executives remain my friends today.

Maybe you think the limos, burgers, and champagne were extravagant. In fact, my cost was under $500 for a chance at a piece of business that would generate $25,000. Little did I know it would culminate in a gift of $75,000 for an evening of entertainment. My client—and now friend—hired The Spinners musical group to perform for a convention I was chairing. My wife is still talking about The Spinners coming up to our suite after the show. She had a once-in-a-lifetime opportunity to sing several songs with the band on a karaoke machine we had in the room.

Here's another example. Two senior meeting planners from Nike were coming to my office to discuss their convention's transportation needs. I had no special relationship with Michael Jordan or any other NBA, NFL, or MLB player, so I needed to dream a little. Our vice president of marketing and vice president of operations brought the planners into our conference room and served them coffee. Minutes later, I arrived in my best tuxedo—and a brand-new pair of Nike high-tops. These shoes were their latest available to the public, and I had shelled out $150 for them, a pair of shoes I do not believe I ever wore again.

The bottom line?

We received their contract and provided them with excellent service during their convention. Investing $150 for a return of over $15,000? A more than reasonable expenditure.

Here is one last story. You may find it a little strange, but I have been called much worse, and I think it goes to the very heart of networking. During my ten years in the hospitality industry, I was proud to have The Coca-Cola Company as a client. I always felt that having a portion of Coca-Cola's business was the Good Housekeeping Seal of Approval for my company, and I took the relationship very seriously.

My wife and I booked a last-minute brief vacation during 1985. Two days before our scheduled departure, I received a telephone call from one of my clients at Coca-Cola. Robert Woodruff, chairman of the board, had died earlier in the day. My client wanted me to know, so I could be ready for what we both assumed would be a large volume of business over the next few days. I told my wife that the trip might need to be put on hold as I contacted every transportation company in Atlanta and throughout the Southeast to have every available limousine ready. The next day, my Coca-Cola contact called to tell me he had no news yet, but those details would be forthcoming. At this point, I had no choice. I love my wife, but there would be other opportunities for vacations. This was The Coca-Cola Company, and I needed to be in Atlanta. We cancelled the trip.

I think it was around eight o'clock the evening before Mr. Woodruff's funeral when my contact next called.

They would need no limousines.

For a moment, I thought my misspent youth listening to Led Zeppelin and the Rolling Stones at full volume had finally taken its toll on my hearing.

"Beg pardon?" I said into the phone. "I thought I heard you say that you would not need any limousines for tomorrow."

"That's right. An edict just arrived from Mr. Roberto Goizueta's office. In deference to Mr. Woodruff's dislike of limousines and grandiose displays of affluence, no one should book or arrive in a limousine at his funeral."

I did receive an order for a single limousine to pick up a well-known newsperson coming from New York to cover the funeral. But that was it. I don't know whom I hated calling more, the eight or nine regional limousine companies whose cars I had on hold—or my wife. I called her first because I was positive that I had no interest in moving in with any of the other guys. If she was angry, however, she never showed it. As usual, she was nothing but understanding. As for me, sure, I was upset about the missed vacation, the business I didn't get, and about having reserved limousines from a lot of good competitors, who were also my friends.

But I was never upset with The Coca-Cola Company. *They* hadn't asked me to do what I did. I did it because *I* valued *them* as a client. It was an investment, and even though it didn't pay off at the time, this world is not about me or about you. It is always about the person in front of us. I knew I had done the right thing.

One short footnote: The Coca-Cola Company celebrated its 100th anniversary in 1986. Would any one like to guess which transportation company coordinated the event and picked up a six-figure engagement? Perhaps the gold-plated Coca-Cola bottle in the shadow box that was given after the event as a "Thank You" gift, which now sits on my credenza, might give you a little hint.

Managing the Time

The time I spend one-on-one with a potential client in his or her office is precious, and I must use that time wisely. But sometimes, no matter how brilliantly I think I am coming across or how well my new suit fits, the prospect is distracted. It may be the third telephone call she just *has* to answer, it may be her assistant coming in and dropping notes on her desk every few minutes, or it may just be the blank stare that betrays a wandering or worrying mind. When I sense that we have lost contact with one another, I stop the conversation and say, "You seem a little distracted. I am sure you have a lot of things on your mind this afternoon. What if I slip out and schedule another appointment through your assistant for a few weeks from now?"

I am sitting in front of a powerful person, but I have no idea if her company is having cash flow problems, her husband is leaving her, or her oldest child has been diagnosed with a horrible disease. On the other hand, maybe it's nothing more dire than an impending visit from her mother-in-law. Whatever is going on, I have sensed that she is not really present for me, and rather than drone on, I seize the opportunity to show a degree of sensitivity that can help win a friend. Sometimes my suggestion evokes an instant apology and an invitation to continue. Sometimes, my prospect takes me up on the offer to reschedule. But even if I have a pledge of undivided attention, I try to reschedule another meeting. If I get out while the getting is good, I leave without a *no*, and I have the hope of getting a better shot another time.

As we discussed earlier, *no* does not always mean no, and, even when it does, it is not the end of the world. There is no reason you should let this little monosyllable stop your heart. I have never had a firing squad come to get me after the *no* was pronounced. If I believe that *no* has come because I have not explained my proposition very well, I may push back a little and try to clarify the potential client's objection. If he or she pushes back harder, however, I know it is time to pack up my belongings and head for the door.

"Thank you for your time. You know, I did not come here to make a sale, but to meet you. I hoped to convince you that I want to help your business be more successful and watch you grow. Any sale that may occur is a byproduct of our working together. If you believe I am telling the truth, you will always see you and me sitting on the same side of the negotiation table. If we are allies, we will never negotiate by trying to cut each other's throat to save a dime. We are focused on helping each other win, and that is how a good relationship should work."

Communicate on a Meaningful Level and Often

I do not enjoy mass mailings, receiving telemarketing calls, or having Spam e-mail fill my in-box. In this, am I different from you? More to the point, am I different from your prospects? The fact is that I go out of my way *not* to buy from a firm that has attempted to reach me by any mass-production means. I receive many Christmas cards every year, as I imagine you do. Can you describe the three best cards you received last year? I know I can't, but I *can* tell you about a few that included a personal picture or story about the family or person who sent the card. If you can't take the time to make your greeting cards personal, save yourself the stamp. Those I receive that bear a printed signature or a printed company name with nothing personal added, I throw into the trash. Why? Because they are meaningless. I buy a few boxes of Christmas cards every year. I send them to my special friends, clients, and loved ones, each with a personal note. The thousands of people in my database to whom I did not send a card never missed it, and I am positive I have not offended them. In fact, whether they know it or not, I helped them avoid additional clutter in their lives.

There are many other ways to create a deeper relationship. Hallmark has a card to celebrate an occasion or feeling for every single day of the year. I ensure that my database is full of the important dates in the lives of all my contacts. I make it a practice to send an anniversary card to each of my key married contacts. I send it not to the office, but to the contact's home. When the spouse opens the card and reads my message, he or she is usually impressed and shares the card with his or her significant other. If you can win the hearts and minds of the spouse or children of your prospect, I promise you are more than halfway toward creating a long and productive relationship. How do I know this? Because it works this way in my house, and it is only reasonable to assume it does in others. In addition, I keep boxes of cards in my desk drawer for birthdays, sympathy, congratulations, thank you, and even just thinking-of-you cards. I write cards when I see or feel a need. If I had to *drive* to Hallmark to buy a card every time I had the urge, I would almost certainly fail to act on my instinct. By keeping a stock of cards handy, I make it easy to follow up on my own best impulses.

Do these cards, kindnesses and sharing a positive message make a difference to those you love and serve? Without question!

Earlier this year, I received a call from a dear friend, fellow Leadership Atlanta alum and a former client of mine, Ms. Julie Untener. She told me about her eighty-nine-year-old mother, Ruth, who is going through breast cancer. Ruth has led a long and fulfilling life and, as a result, decided to refuse treatment. She is at peace with her life and health situation. What a very fortunate place of peace for anyone to be in at any stage of life! Julie told me that she appreciated my positive notes and musings I post from time to time through greeting cards, emails, and on social media. Julie then asked if I would be willing to write her mother a card to cheer her up and to encourage her as she goes through this transition. I do not recall a moment of humility quite as powerful as that one in my life. To think that this lovely person, who also went through breast cancer earlier in her own life, was asking me to do this filled me with deep joy. I have written my new "Ohio surrogate mom" three times as of today, July 19, 2022, and I will write her again the first week of August. Each time her mom receives a card from "Julie's friend," who she has never seen or spoken to, she immediately calls Julie to share the message.

Once, Julie was visiting her mom when the card arrived, and they read it together. Just knowing this is happening gives me more happiness than any I have received from making a sale, winning an award, or receiving positive press. Only three people in the world would know this story if Julie had not agreed to allow me to share it with you. Thank you, Julie, for allowing me to make this much more personal for the readers of this book.

On another note, and for a variety of reasons, Julie and I have not done any business with one another in over eight years and may not ever do business together again. Julie's role at NCR has changed, and I am moving toward the end of my career. As I have shared many times in this book, this principle is crucial to all I am sharing with you. The heart of networking has absolutely nothing to do with business or sales. The gift Julie gave to me by inviting me to write her mom is more valuable than all the commissions I have earned over fifty-five-plus years in sales.

Communication is about more than generating new business. It is the means of maintaining relationships. Companies spend millions of dollars attempting to win business, but they spend a mere fraction of this amount to maintain their current customers. Yet, as every experienced businessperson knows, your best customers are always your current customers. The cost of replacing a lost customer is astronomical, and it would not be necessary at all if a reasonable effort were made to ensure that current customers feel appreciated. When was the last time you called your top ten clients for no reason other than to say hello or offer to buy them a cup of coffee? Most of us call our clients only when we need a sale. Then and only then do they loom as our easiest targets. But if they only hear from you when you've got your hand out, they'll learn to think of you not as a friend but as a peddler. Don't make a call just to make a sale. Call to maintain a friendship.

Create Additional Value

There are many other ways to keep yourself before your contacts. You must continue the learning process throughout your life. Should you ever decide that you have learned enough, have a good friend or your spouse call the local funeral director to come pick up your body. You are dead regardless of whether you are aware of that fact. What you know and what you learn on an ongoing basis creates a treasure you can share with your contacts. It ensures that you can always give value, even if you don't always make a sale.

I was a very poor student. I had little interest in the subjects being taught and even less personal discipline where class work was concerned. What I did have was a passion for reading about people, places, and things, both local and international. One of the few tests I passed in history in either my junior or senior year was the annual *"Time-Life Current Events Test."* In fact, I scored among the top three or four on this test in both my junior and senior years. My history teacher said she wished I would put the same effort into the rest of the class, but I was bored and could never concentrate much on my schoolwork. It was not until I was middle aged that testing revealed I am ADD/ADHD. With apologies to Barbara Mandrel and her 1980s hit about country music, "I was ADD before ADD was cool." Back then most people just thought I had the attention span of a strobe light, which, by the way, was a hugely popular party accessory in the late sixties and early seventies.

Nevertheless, a love of current events has been a constant in my life. I want to know more about Iraq, India, and the Middle East than how my Falcons, Braves, and the Georgia BullDawgs are doing. (Though I want to know that, too.) As importantly, I want to be able to fully discuss why Black Lives Matter and why when discussing human and civil rights I must, as a white businessperson, make a stand because in my opinion, "White Silence = White Consent. I Refuse to Be Silent."

My idea of a vacation used to be getting up early, buying three or four newspapers, going to the beach with them, and not coming back until I've read them all. Today, I don't have to go buy the newspapers, I have daily subscriptions to the *Atlanta Journal-Constitution, Columbus Ledger, Washington Post, The New York Times,* and the *Atlanta Business Chronicle* all arriving to my inbox before I start my day. My mania for current events ensures that I am amply stocked with up-to-date information, and this, in turn, has allowed me to help countless clients and friends by supplying them with the right information at the right time.

Many years ago, I had greeting cards printed with two different messages: "In the News" and "Thought this might be of some interest."

My name was printed on the inside, and each card included a flap to hold an article clipping. I always maintained a stock of these special cards, and every time my assistant or I saw something relating to a contact or client, we clipped it, put it in a card, I scribbled a brief personal note, and dropped it in the mail. What can the person who receives this think other than, "That was thoughtful. I can see Steele is really interested in me and not just in getting my business." Point, set, and match. Today, I no longer have a stock of cards or clip articles, but I still do the same thing—usually by sending a link to the article.

Nothing in business is more valuable than relevant information. Stock your mind with it, and you become a walking, talking treasure. At cocktail parties and business events, you have the powerful and impressive advantage of being able to keep up with, join, or even lead almost any conversation. Beginning a conversation by asking somebody for his opinion on the local tax hike, foreign policy, or the price of peas in Peoria is far more meaningful than "How about the weather?" or that old seventies standby, "What's your sign?"

In Atlanta, the most widely read business publication is the weekly *Atlanta Business Chronicle*. I have been reading the *Chronicle* since 1981 or 1982. Over the 1990s and early 2,000s, I used to go to the Kroger close to my house at 5:30 a.m. every Friday morning. I would go in and buy a copy of the *Atlanta Business Chronicle* as soon as the truck dropped them off. I would then spend a little time in the parking lot skimming the paper. If I saw a mention of a friend or one of my clients, I grabbed my cell phone, called their office, and left a 5:45 a.m. voice mail congratulating them on the mention or story in the *Chronicle*. The only negative to this tactic is if you happen to call someone who forwards cell or office calls to the home phone. I dare not print the comments I received one morning when a spouse picked up, questioned my sanity, and then my manhood. However, even in this instance, I received a call back later in the day asking me how I knew the story was in the *Chronicle*.

"The reporter said the story might be there, but my copy doesn't get here until the afternoon!"

"That's what I'm here for," I replied.

If I saw a story or a picture particularly flattering to a client, I would go back into the store and buy five more copies. Later, I would I stop by Krispy Kreme Donuts to pick up several dozen of the regular "Hot" glazed ones and deliver two dozen along with several *Chronicles*, all opened to the relevant story to my client's office.

I don't do that any longer because now the *Chronicle* is available online and at midnight Thursday evening/Friday morning, the paper is available to read online. I then go through the same procedure by calling or texting my friend to tell them about the great article in to-morrow's *Chronicle*. Until Covid-19 took over our lives, later that morning, I visited Krispy Kreme to buy donuts and to Kroger to buy *Chronicles* before visiting them to drop off my gifts. I will restart that process now that Covid-19 has slowed its roll and I have both vaccinations and both boosters.

Information doesn't have to be delivered to your client or prospect in a newspaper clipping or a midnight email. Draw on your mental stock and begin your conversation with a few facts you know to be directly relevant to your contact's situation. People may or may not be interested in you and what you have to sell, but they are always interested in themselves and whatever affects them. Just make sure you are brief and to the point and, in all cases, absolutely truthful. Don't even think about finessing or faking information. Not only is this plain wrong, the downside of being discovered as a fraud is far steeper than any temporary advantage you might gain from "getting over" on a prospect or client.

And what if you just don't know anything about this person or her company? In that case, ask yourself: Why did I choose her as a candidate for a meeting?

You have only one shot at a first impression. If you are not willing to do the work in networking, stay home and be good to your spouse and children. As a networker, your goal is to get your prospects to open up and for them to see that you really do know who they are and what at least some of their problems are. Your purpose in meeting with them is not to share how smart and talented you are, but to listen as they tell you how smart and talented *they* are. Do that, and they end up with respect for your brains and ability. President Theodore Roosevelt said: "People do not care how much you know, until they know how much you care." I would add: "How much you care about them."

Listen, listen, and listen some more, but when the questions come about *you* and *your* company, be prepared with an expanded version of the elevator pitch we discussed earlier. Make it to the point and positive but leave no loose ends.

Take Your Time

I have stressed the importance of making every minute of your meeting time count. *That* is the essence of delivering real value, both to your prospect or client and to you. However, don't try to pack everything into a single meeting. Don't shoot for love at first sight. Business relationships are much like courtship. They cannot be rushed. Any relationship worth being part of is worth cultivating over time. I confess that I have lived most of my life believing the adage, "Rome was not built in a day because I was not the general contractor." As a result of this misguided belief, I'm sure I've missed a lot of great relationships, not to mention quality time with my wife and children. Don't make the same mistake. I now understand—and it is worth remembering—that although the early bird may get the worm, it is the second mouse who gets the cheese.

Be Willing to Invest in Your Career

I believe that to be successful, you must invest in your career. Reading this book is part of such an investment. You also invest by becoming a general student of the world. Learning is a powerful tool. Skimming several newspapers, online publications, and industry journals every day will help you get the latest information of importance to your prospects and clients. You cannot believe the fanfare you'll receive when, during the middle of a conversation, you drop onto the desk a copy of an article pertinent to the discussion. At that moment, you are elevated from salesperson to counselor and consultant.

Sometimes your investment must take the form of cold, hard cash. I have been an entrepreneur most of my career, and I have spent tens of thousands of dollars attempting to win business. I am sure I wasted some along the way, and I am even surer my former partners would agree. I have been an entrepreneur-in-residence for two companies that are the world's largest in their respective industries. Of course, I did not have an unlimited budget to use in winning business, and when my budget started to pinch in a given month or quarter, I could have sat at my desk all day and pouted. I could have blamed a lack of sales on the mean old corporate machine. But I did no such thing. Instead, whenever I thought it necessary, I personally paid for tickets to rock concerts, coffee mugs with our company logo, flowers in sympathy for the loss of a client's loved one, and parking for clients who visited our office. Over a five-year period, these personal expenditures ran into the tens of thousands. I am confident that I have invested north of $100,000 of my personal net worth in entertaining clients and donating money to causes they personally support. I may never know if the investment was productive dollar for dollar, but I do know that I felt good about making it each and every time. The day I quit doing that I have either finally retired or you can find Richard E. Steele, Jr. in the obituary column of the *Atlanta Journal Constitution*.

My wife can tell you about investments we made in my career when I did not have a job or any income after a business failure in 1998. Those expenditures were hard to justify, but I believe they were the key to my receiving a great consulting assignment and eventually being hired at Pricewaterhouse Coopers. In early 2000, I heard a major technology executive tell a story about an especially audacious investment. He began his story by asking how many of us had ever received a letter in the mail with one or two dollars enclosed, asking us to fill out a form or call an 800 number. It seems that everyone in the room had received such a letter at some time or other. He continued: "A few months ago, I received a letter from a company asking for a meeting. The letter included a *one-hundred-dollar* bill. Now, in the past, I always put the dollar or two in my pocket and threw the letter in the trash. But this one was different. I was taken by this bold approach. I called the company and set up an appointment. I listened to the pitch, and, at the end of the presentation, I asked the two executives if they minded my asking a few questions. I wanted to know how they had come up with this promotion and how it was working.

"Their reply was 'We have tried every marketing medium that is available. We are trying to get to a select few key executives who are very hard to reach. We have spent a lot of money trying to reach them without any real results. We began using this a few months ago. Our rate of response is 70 percent. That makes it the most effective promotion we have ever used. The best part is that recouping our investment doesn't require many of that 70 percent to buy. When the right few people buy, we not only recoup our investment on all the mailings but also make a profit for our company.

"My second question was this: 'Is there any downside to this and, if so, what?'

"The salesman said, 'Obviously, it hurts to invest $100 each on the 30 percent who don't ever return our call. I think we also run the risk of alienating some people, who may think this approach is crass or offensive, as if we believe we can buy their business or friendship. However, on the positive side, the executives who do call already know we are willing to invest our company's money, time, and energy to get to know them. I believe they think we are creative and that we have already researched their company as a potential partner—or we would not have sent the gift.'"

In the end, the teller of this tale did not buy from the company, but he did give them the thirty minutes they had requested. He also had a new idea to try for his own company. Most people spend hours, days, and months figuring out what to give clients for Christmas or trying to determine just the right way to influence a potential client. Forget about the money for the moment. Calculate the value of the relationship. If I have a client spending $200,000 annually with a 30 percent gross profit margin, why would I even think about spending $100 for a Steak House gift certificate? That just does not cut it. I *should* be taking my client and his top two or three executives to a Braves, Hawks, or Falcon's game or a great outdoor concert at Atlanta's Chastain Park. The cost for the evening could well top $1,000 or more, but it will be remembered and appreciated much longer than any gift certificate. I doubt the receiver of the gift certificate remembers the giver before or after he takes his first bite.

Spending money on a substantial gift is impressive, but even more memorable is your demonstration of creativity in selecting the gift. This is typically judged as a measure of how you rate your client's value to your company. If I can discover what especially interests my client or prospect, then deciding on the gift becomes easier. I have bought many $200 bottles of wine as gifts, even though I have never spent $20 for one I intend to drink. The folks at the local tobacco shop wonder how I've escaped lung cancer, since I buy six or seven $300 boxes of cigars each year. I have never smoked a single cigar out of any of those boxes, but I think I have had the same kind of pleasure when I see a client open a box. I savor the aroma of joy when clients call to tell me they are sitting by their pool or riding in their sports car enjoying one of the cigars. How many of your clients ever thank you for your gift, much less call you while they are enjoying it? It is all about being personal in a genuine way.

You don't have to persuade your valued contacts that you are their best friend, but you do have to demonstrate how you value them and their business. Many of us find it hard to part with a dollar as an investment in ourselves. How much harder is investing *your* money in gifts or other items for someone else or someone else's company! But that is part of giving value to the people with whom you do business, and, therefore, it is also part of investing in yourself. Networking requires that you always see the bigger picture. Value costs—in time, effort, and cash. Keep your focus on the value rather than the cost.

10

■

Food for Thought

NAPOLEON SAID THAT AN ARMY TRAVELS ON ITS STOMACH. So do net-workers—at least the savvy ones. Read any book on etiquette, and it will tell you that hovering around the buffet table is not good form. You're supposed to collect your food on a little plate, then retreat with it into the crowd. This is not advice I ever follow. Instead, whenever I attend any event, I make it my business to spend a *lot* of time around the food station. Now, I'm talking about the *food* station.

I've learned that hanging around the *bar* is interesting for the first hour or so, but, after that, very little intelligent conversation occurs. Is it any wonder?

In contrast, it is at the food station where real creativity begins. Food has always been a great starter of conversation and the building of community. I am sure some of your fondest memories are of family reunions, church picnics, and company outings where there was more food than the law should allow. Think of the last time you attended a party at the home of a friend. No matter how beautiful or spacious the house, no matter how thoughtfully the host and hostess had prepared and decorated it for the occasion, 90 percent of the guests spent 90 percent of their time crowded into the kitchen, sharing food and fellowship. It is only human. Where the food is, there also is the action.

Just Watching

A lot of people assume that a successful networker has to be an aggressive gladhander, who wades into the crowd, grabs people by the lapels, and is always talking, talking, talking. In fact, I try to spend as much of the early part of any event standing in a corner as out of the way as possible. As the great Hall of Fame baseball player, coach, and creator of iconic malapropisms Yogi Berra once said, "You can observe a lot just by watching."

I want to gauge the mood of the crowd, to pick up on the buzz and feel the vibe. I want to scope out just where the action is and who is receiving a great deal of attention from other attendees. I want to identify the center of each conversational group. People vote with their feet, the old saying goes, and watching just where and when groups cluster is a graphic indication of who the real leaders are. I want a feel for where the most promising and productive potential contacts are. Of almost equal importance, I need to see where the people to avoid may be lurking. I cannot afford to be shanghaied into a waste of a valuable event.

More Food

A committed networker identifies and attends as many relevant events as possible. Depending on where you are and what your business is, this can make truly terrific demands on your time. Demanding as event attendance may be, however, you should be doing even more. I don't wait for someone to throw a party or stage an event before I start networking. I create my own occasions.

On a typical day, before Covid-19, I might have two or three breakfast meetings and two lunches in addition to a dinner, or reception. I might maintain such a schedule three or even four days during any given week. I tell myself that this is the only way I can achieve my ideal body weight. Unfortunately, I have personally determined that, at six-three, I am still eleven inches shorter than the published height/weight charts say I should be.

Why do I put myself through such grueling days? My daughter (she was nineteen at the time) used to say I do it to "See my peeps," which I think meant that it's the best way I can meet and visit with friends, contacts, and clients. I have a different favorite restaurant for each meal of the day, but I always favor places that are like the bar in the classic television show *Cheers,* places "where everybody knows your name." You will be amazed by how impressed your guests are when everyone—hostess, manager, and servers—greets you warmly by name.

During the height of the dot-com mania in the late 1990s, I had a favorite restaurant for breakfast that I would visit no fewer than four mornings a week. Every major Atlanta publication and two national technology magazines have featured me networking in my booth, where they claimed a lot of what was happening in the technology community was happening. It is hard to buy that kind of publicity just for eating a meal. My record for a single day is sitting down at 6:15 a.m. and leaving the restaurant at 3:30 p.m. This span of nine hours and fifteen minutes represents seven different meetings. While my mind was stimulated by the company and several dozen cups of coffee, fighting the fanny fatigue would have been tough work for anyone.

It is a good strategy to hold your meetings in the same places because you will usually receive the best service if you become known as a regular. Think about your own business. You are willing to go farther out of the way for a regular customer than for a first-timer. While it is human nature and good business to treat repeat customers very, very well, I see the relationship as a two-way street. Over the years, I have given small Christmas gifts to any number of the servers who treat me like a regular. Indeed, we have created a relationship over time, and I consider these people my partners in providing "our" guest with an enjoyable meal and an atmosphere conducive to a productive conversation.

Your server can be instrumental in setting the mood and can even help you make a point or two, provided you work as a team. Much success in networking, as in life, is in no small part based on the actions of the people who surround you. It makes sense, then, to go out of your way to get to know someone who will be chatting with you and your prospects three or four mornings a week.

I am also a generous tipper. I don't say that to brag, but to suggest that it is simply good, ethical business. If I take a table for four or five hours, conduct several meetings, but generate a check that's no more than $50 or so—mostly in coffee—how can I justify tipping $7.50 or even 20 percent, a whopping ten dollars? I have taken the table from a hard-working person who would otherwise have served four or five groups spending much more money than I. You don't always have to spend big bucks for admission to a special networking event, and you don't always have to overwhelm your contact with a lavishly expensive dinner, but you should never treat any networking venue as a free ride. The gratuity I give reflects my idea of fair rent on the table or booth. It is important, it is right, it creates a legitimately happy relationship with the server, and it will allow you to present yourself to your prospect or client as an honorable businessperson committed to giving fair value for fair value received.

11

■

Owning Your Contacts

NETWORKING EVENTS NEVER GO JUST ONE WAY, supplying an endless stream of new contacts. Very often, people I hardly know approach me to ask for an introduction to one of my clients or good friends. This presents me with a dilemma. I know *they* know that I have a relationship with the person in question, but what I do *not* know is what they hope to accomplish by my introduction.

I *own* my contacts. Now that does not give me any rights concerning them, but it does give me serious responsibilities, including the responsibility to protect their privacy. The relationship my contacts represent is, in a word, sacred. It is built on a foundation of trust, and it is my responsibility to do nothing that will erode that foundation. This is my obligation, sacred and absolute, to my contact. In contrast, I have no obligation to a casual acquaintance who asks me for an introduction.

An Explanation and an Opportunity

Well, maybe I do owe this person something. At least, *I* feel I do. I owe him an explanation and an opportunity.

"Ricky," the acquaintance asks, "can you introduce me to Mr. Smith? You know him, right?"

"Yes," I respond, "I do know Bob. Bob is a great guy and one of the real leaders in his field. As you are aware if you have been trying to contact him, he is a very busy man. I am as protective of him as I would be of you if the situation were reversed. How about sharing your elevator pitch with me? I am ready to give you my undivided attention now, if you like."

Asking for this person's elevator pitch takes some of my time, of course, and, at networking events, nothing is more valuable than my time. However, listening to what he's got to say will allow me to judge if my contact might be interested in a meeting. If it is clear from the pitch that he would be interested, terrific! I now have an opportunity to offer a valuable contact to *my* contact—while making a new friend in the process. If, however, it is apparent that meeting this person will be a waste of my contact's time, I need to know. Bob really *is* a very busy person, but he is also someone who is gracious enough to take my calls as well as my referrals. If I send Bob four or five people a week who are not good fits for him or his company, how long will it be before my calls go unreturned? Even worse, what if I make the introduction, and this person, who looks like a nice enough guy, takes Bob and his company for a ride? Maybe he's an outright fraud, or maybe he's just incompetent. In either case, Bob will know that I *meant* him no harm, but he is bound to be far less open to me and to whomever I might send his way in the future.

Now, I want to make myself clear. The point is that you need to take ownership of your contacts. Protect them. Don't give away introductions just for the asking. However, it is also a mistake to act the role of the miser and hoard your relationship with your client. Effective networking requires that you not only obtain introductions, but that, when appropriate, you make them as well. If you judge that your contact can profit by an introduction, make it. This judgment is always easier to make when the person who asks for the introduction is someone you know well, someone whose product or service is very familiar to you. Don't hesitate to endorse people and products in which you truly believe. And make your endorsement count by being specific about it. Don't just say Sarah Jones is a "wonderful person"; give an example of something great you know she did for another client. It is in everyone's interest to promote quality work and top-notch service. Not only will this help Sarah Jones, it will also benefit your contact—and, of course, it will be good for you, who has once again demonstrated that you are helpful, full of good judgment and great advice, and a problem solver.

Know When to Say No

My life goal and ambition is to try to help everyone I meet, regardless of what they have done for me in the past or might possibly do for me in the future. This does not mean that I always say yes when I am asked for help.

Sometimes all I need to hear is the elevator pitch to decide whether to make a requested introduction. Sometimes, however, the pitch is not complete enough to allow me to decide on the spot one way or the other. In this case, I'll tell the person seeking the introduction that his proposition sounds interesting, but "I need to do some follow-up research before I bring you and Bob together. What is your company website URL?"

At this point, the person has two choices. He can tell me, either politely or not, to forget about it, or he can furnish me with sources of information as well as the names of satisfied clients willing to endorse him and his company. In the first case, that's an end to it. There will be no introduction. In the second case, there is every indication that this is a serious, committed person. Chances are that my follow-up research will yield a positive picture about him and his company, in which case I'll call him up and tell him that I'm pleased to make the introduction he's asked for. But if I discover that this person's company is not known for quality, or if I find that the references provided just don't check out, I'll still call him—but it will be to tell him, politely, that I cannot make the introduction.

It is not always easy to explain the reasons for declining the request. I usually just say that "I have followed up on the information you gave me, and your company isn't a good fit for Bob." Most of the time, that ends it. However, if I am pressed for a further explanation, I tell the truth as politely but straightforwardly as I can. It would, of course, be easier to lie and say that "I ran this by Bob, and he had no interest." Maybe such a lie will be the end of the story. But then, maybe this person will find someone else to introduce him to Bob. He and Bob will talk, and during the conversation my lie will be discovered. The result? I'll be branded as a liar. My relationship with Bob, built on trust, will crumble—and because Bob is part of my network and has his own networks, word will get around that I can't be trusted. Now my business will fall into deep jeopardy. Lies almost always come back to haunt you.

Little white lies are never little and certainly not white. At best, they're a dirty gray. You may never come away clean.

Beck and Call

I believe that the sales process has a beginning but is without end. Once you receive an order, your new client and his or her company should become part of your waking thoughts and your nighttime prayers. Your clients should believe and know that you are looking out for their best interest in everything you do, and not just pertaining to this one order. I promise my potential clients that once they do business with me, I am at their beck and call. Nothing is out of the question, provided it is legal and ethical. If they recognize something I can help them with—whether it is public relations, tickets to a concert, placing articles in the press, or obtaining introductions to potential clients for their company—I invite and I want them to call me.

Several years ago, when I was a search executive for Korn/Ferry International, I received a call from the CEO of one of Atlanta's newer and most exciting technology companies. They were going to conduct a search for a new VP of marketing. From my company, I assembled a team of experts who had great experience in the prospective client's field. We wanted to get to know the client company intimately, so we invited the entire management team out to a rather expensive dinner. Later, we spent three hours in their headquarters learning more about their company and what they specifically needed in a marketing VP.

The management team seemed very interested in our value proposition, especially my offer to introduce them to new client opportunities. We also discussed a few companies with which I had relationships, and they were properly impressed.

I have always been guilty of counting my chickens before they come home to roost, and I would have bet my house on earning their search. Imagine my disappointment when, about a week later, the CEO called to say that he was very sorry, but they had chosen a small boutique search firm.

Disappointed? I was stunned.

He explained that his main reason for going with the competing firm was that they were charging about $5,000 less than we were on a $60,000 search. By a little less than 10 percent, we had lost to a firm with fewer than six employees—total. In contrast, we had dedicated to this single search six people, full time, from our Atlanta staff of over sixty. I admit that, along with my disappointment, I also began sweating about how I was going to justify to my boss a $550 dinner for a non-client.

Without taking the telephone receiver from my ear, I bit my tongue, counted rapidly to ten, said a short prayer, and then told the CEO that I honestly could not understand his decision, based on all we had to offer. But, I concluded, "You are the CEO, it was your decision to make, and I wish you the best of luck. If there is anything we can do for you in the future, we would love the opportunity to compete again."

Almost a year later, I received a call from this same CEO, who asked me if I knew a certain executive with a Fortune 500 company in Colorado. Of course, he already knew that the executive in question was a dear friend and, indeed, a mentor of mine.

"Sure, I know him," I replied. "He is one of the finest people I know, and I think the world of him, his wife, and his son." In fact, I had dinner with him and his wife in Denver just a few weeks earlier.

The CEO then popped the question: "Would you introduce me to him? Our product would be a perfect fit for his operation. Just get us in, and we'll do the rest."

Chutzpah is not a word I had learned in Columbus, Georgia, but I knew what it meant, and it seemed to me this guy had it in staggering abundance. It took me a moment or two to compose myself before I could finally utter, "Let me think about it for a day or two and give you a call back."

I did not tell my boss about this exchange for a whole day, because I just could not talk about it. The next day, however, my boss and I sat down and discussed the implications. I was personal friends with two of the venture capitalists who had invested in the CEO's company, which made the situation even more complicated. I finally e-mailed the CEO with this message: "I appreciate your calling me for my help. I am sure you recall my attempt to secure your search work just a year ago. I tried my best to win your trust at that time, and, as part of my sales process, I shared with you that my personal key value proposition over my competition was my ability to get you into places no one else could. I only have so many of those kinds of relationships, and if I begin calling my friends too often, I will become a nuisance and lose the right to get through. It would be unfair to my current clients and to my company if I use one of these favors to help a non-client. If in the future you need additional search work, please give me a chance and the offer to introduce you to my friend will still stand." I did not feel good about doing this, but it was the right thing to do for my clients and my company. Most important, I had to be honest.

I received an e-mail reply within minutes: "Ricky, I do understand. I was too embarrassed to even ask you for this favor, but the Board and key management want this to happen, and they urged me to give you a call. I look forward to seeing you at an event around town soon."

Did he ever call me to do a search? No. But about six months later, one of the venture capitalists in the company did call me and hired Korn/Ferry to execute a search for a new CEO. How much do you think that "saved" $5,000 actually cost the company—and the CEO—over the long run?

Being a generous, ethical networker does not require you to become a doormat. You've worked hard to make your contacts and to turn them into trusted friends. You don't have to give them away to people who haven't earned them. Business is not charity. It is the exchange of value for value. When people focus on cost instead of value, they almost always make a bad bargain, one that is sometimes far worse than they could ever have imagined. Offer value, and deal in value.

12
■
Secrets of Networking
Up the Food Chain

THE MOST EXPERIENCED, MOST SAVVY NETWORKERS HAVE developed a sixth sense about the people they approach. They home in on precisely the individuals who have the power to buy from them. Sometimes the choice is obvious, and they go straight for the CEO. But in many organizations, the CEO does not make the buying decision that may be most relevant to you. Effective CEOs are by definition great delegators, and the difference between delegating and micromanaging is avoiding intervention in tasks more properly assigned to subordinates. So, very often, the networker needs to identify the person at just the right level, neither too high nor too low, and approach him or her. This can be a delicate and complicated task. A good rule of thumb is, when in doubt, aim one level higher than you guess necessary. It is always easier to network downward in the corporate food chain than it is to move up.

Of course, in many cases, you have little choice. It is all well and good to talk about aiming at this level or that, but, as the old saying goes, "the best is the enemy of the good," and if you are at an event that presents a golden opportunity to meet a second- or third-tier manager of Acme Widgets, you are not likely to pass this up in the distant hope of a chance meeting, someday, with the CEO. Once you establish a relationship with this lower-level manager, you have at least gained entry into the organization, and you may be able to work your way up to your target level. In some cases, a lower-level relationship works very well until you feel that your relationship with the company has matured to the point that the time has come to establish a relationship with management at a higher level.

For various reasons, then, you will sooner or later need to network to a higher level than your original contact. The hard truth is that, in most organizations, this is not so easy.

Shooting Low, Aiming High

Lewis Grizzard was a great Southern humorist, who died much too young. My favorite Grizzard book is *They Tore Out My Heart and Stomped That Sucker Flat*, about Lewis's open-heart surgery. I read it to my dad the night before his own open-heart surgery in Birmingham, Alabama, back in the mid-1980s. We both laughed so hard the nurses came in to see if we were drinking. But if that is my favorite Grizzard book, my favorite single one of his stories is titled "Shoot Low, Boys, They're Riding Shetland Ponies." It's a title that should ring bells for any networker. We have to shoot low when we find ourselves looking into the eyes of an available target who happens not to be the final decision maker in an organization.

Remember: *The best is the enemy of the good.* Establishing *some* relationship is substantially better than having *no* relationship at all. But we cannot stop with knowing only people at the levels below those at which the decisions are made. Cultivate the lower-level relationship. Provide value, and, many times, it will be the lower-echelon people who help you climb higher up the ladder. After all, if you impress or serve their boss well, it naturally reflects positively on them.

I will not make a cold call on a decision maker until I have established a relationship with someone who has a relationship with him or her. The most obvious candidate is, of course, the person we met when we aimed low, the one who works with and reports to the ultimate decision maker. If I have done my job well establishing a relationship with this person, he or she will feel confident about making an introduction higher up. At this point, although I don't yet have my hands on a red-hot prospect, the situation has at least ceased to be a cold call.

Perhaps there comes to mind just now an obvious image: the steppingstone. We use the figure of speech all the time. "Joe took the job at XYZ Company as a *steppingstone* to the job he *really* wanted at ABC Company." It is all too easy to think of your lower-level contacts as *steppingstones* to the people you "really" want to get to know. An easy thought, but a very destructive approach.

People are people, not steppingstones. You cannot establish

genuine, honestly productive relationships at a higher level in an organization by mistreating, belittling, or ignoring those with whom you initially established relationships. It's not only hurtful and immoral, it just doesn't work. What goes around really *does* come around. Perhaps you've heard the maxim that it is important to avoid treading on the hands of those you pass on your way up the ladder of success because you will see many of those people later as you make your way down.

As you pursue other paths upward in an organization, never forget your original flag waver. In fact, it is important to try to promote that person's career internally whenever you have the opportunity. This is not just a way of rewarding someone who helped you, it is empowering an ally within an organization that is important to your business. Networking, remember, is about actually and actively *creating* a reality that is most favorable to your business. It's nice if you happen to find a client firm in which everyone happens to know and like you but finding such a company is a pretty long shot. That being the case, do everything within your power to *create* such a client company. Don't forget those at all levels who have helped you and do whatever you can to put them in even better positions to help you. Bear this in mind: In today's business world, the cold call is about as desirable as a polyester leisure suit or a Dodge Gremlin. You can do better. You *must* do better.

Beyond the Obvious

While the most obvious route to the top in any organization may begin by making contact with someone at *some* level within that organization, effective networking also calls for approaches via the less obvious avenues. We must have quality relationships with neighbors, friends, clients, and even vendors who are willing to vouch for us, either to their boss or just generally. You are the sum of all your relationships. That, as far as the world is concerned, is your identity and your reputation.

"Joe is a reliable, talented, and honorable person."

"Who says so?"

Answer that question with "Joe says so," and you will make an infinitely less persuasive case than if you answer, "*Everybody* says so—the CEO at Acme Widgets, the people he volunteers with at the Neighborhood Food Bank, and Jane Doe, who has done business with him for twenty years."

If you cannot immediately find someone on your rung of the corporate ladder in your target firms, begin searching—*everywhere.* You can meet people in service clubs, little league ball games, cheerleading competitions, and just about any other venues where people gather for a common purpose. As I mentioned earlier, volunteering in non-profit organizations is not only a terrific way to serve your community (and yourself as part of that community) but a wonderfully productive way to network with honorable, focused, and productive people who are in the truest sense the pillars of the community. Volunteer work is an excellent foundation for growth. I speak from personal experience. You can accomplish great things by networking in the not-for-profit sphere, and you get the profound personal satisfaction of making the world a better place.

Burn No Bridge

Never forget your original flag waver. This should be your life mantra. And here is another one: *My competitor is not my enemy.*

I have heard the following attributed to several people, including the ancient Chinese military philosopher Sun Tzu, President Lyndon B. Johnson, and Don Vito Corleone in *The Godfather.* "Hold your friends close, and your enemies closer." Whoever said it first, I have always found it very good advice, but not for the same reasons I think were originally intended. When I am able to outsell my competition, he may consider me Public Enemy #1. Just because I am his enemy, however, does not oblige me to make him mine. My job is not to wipe out his business. My job is to sell my product or service. I want to win every time my product is the right fit for my client. As a salesman, I often find myself in competitive situations. I know that if I do not make the sale, it will affect my relationship with my company and will determine whether I make next month's mortgage payment. If my competitor closes up shop, and I therefore win by default, I will take the win. I will feel sorry for him, and I will pray for him and his family. I may even call my former competitor and offer him help in finding a new job. I have lost many times to competitors, and, to date, none have been so grateful that they've offered to help me buy groceries. Some, however, have sent business my way when they knew my company had the better solution for their prospect or when their company was not in a position to fill an order. I've done the same for them.

The English poet Alfred, Lord Tennyson said, "No man ever got very high by pulling other people down. The intelligent merchant does not knock his competitors. The sensible worker does not knock those who work with him. Don't knock your friends. Don't knock your enemies. Don't knock yourself." Competition keeps you and me honest. It keeps us focused, and it should keep us intent on improving our company's offerings. Without competition, companies and individuals get lazy, and the customer loses. Ultimately, we *all* lose, because, in the absence of quality and satisfaction, customers start buying less from everyone, period.

It is important to win business with integrity. You must not misrepresent your company's products, and you must not bad-mouth those of your competitor. This does not mean you cannot compare competing specs, prices, and value. These are facts. But draw the line at character assassination and the like. It may be true that your competitor filed for Chapter 11 several years ago, but this "revelation" should not be in your bag of tricks. The bearer of bad news often finds himself on the wrong end of a shoot-the-messenger mentality. Keep your pitch at the level of fact. There are ways to convey important information to your potential client without coming off as an assassin.

"Mr. Smith," you say to a prospect, "I am sure you are talking to a number of my competitors. You have an important decision to make and one that is going to have a huge impact on your company's future. I highly recommend that you do a thorough background check on each company, including a financial history through Dun and Bradstreet or Equifax. I ask that you please start with my company first. Once you've collected all your data, I'll be happy to come over and answer any questions you may have."

You've taken the high road by maintaining your integrity and trustworthiness. The facts are there for your prospect, if he wants them. You can't force him to do the background check, of course, and, as a result, he may never find out that your competitor declared bankruptcy at one point or is being sued by three clients right now. You might, therefore, fail to win the business. *This time.* However, you can be confident that your approach has gained the attention of this prospect, who may come to you again in the fullness of time and who, for now, will have an interesting—highly positive—story to tell about you and your company to his various contacts in the industry. Not only will the truth be on your side. You'll have reality itself—the very environment within which you do business—pointing positive signs toward you and your enterprise.

Using Humor in Networking

I believe the Bible is a wonderful place for learning whether you believe in God or not. The wisdom that is shared there, especially in Psalms, Proverbs, and Ecclesiastes, has withstood the test of time. Proverbs gives us two good reasons for laughing and making others laugh. In Proverbs 15:15 we learn, "All the days of the oppressed are wretched, but the cheerful heart has a continual feast." Feasting always had more appeal to a solidly built man like me than feeling wretched. Proverbs 17:22 goes further: "A cheerful heart is good medicine, but a crushed spirit dries up the bones."

It does not matter if we have something to be happy about at the moment. We can choose in our hearts to be happy if we are willing to share this happiness with others. Joy and contentment are internal, not external. Humor can break tension and knock down barriers in business or walls separating individuals. Always remember, the butt of any joke or story must be the teller or some inanimate object. Humor that relies on race, creed, color, sexual orientation, or gender may get you a few laughs at the water cooler, but you will alienate most decent people in the world. I hear TV comedians put down other people on a regular basis. I may laugh just from the shock value, but when they are finished, I feel sad. There is no real pleasure in attacking another person's heritage or situation in life. Everyone has problems, everyone has pain. None of us has the power to solve all the problems and pain in the world, but we can provide a measure of relief. I spend hours online each week to scope out new jokes and one-liners. I also collect funny posters and memes. I share the posters along with my commentary on Facebook. A few years ago, I created three regular posts that I try to make each week. They are "Just Another Manic Monday," "Wacky Wednesday," and "Friday Follies." Some weeks I may miss one or two, but I do my best because it is helping others and myself. Often, I receive more positive comments, smiley faces and heart icons from my humorous posts than from the more serious ones. I don't post vulgarity or hit the third rail concerning race, religion, social standing, or anything that could be offensive. Most of the put downs are all pointed to me personally.

Am I ever serious? Not as often as I should be, but then again, as often as I feel led to be. My dad also loved to use humor both at the office and at home, and I do know that his clients and friends always looked forward to his visits. Now that I think about it, I am pretty serious—about humor. In 2006, I enrolled in a humor course given by a great guy who is now a dear friend, Jeff Justice, who has been teaching business executives the power of humor since 1990. After six weeks of classes, the graduation ceremony is a five-minute set at the PunchLine Comedy Club in Atlanta. I had so much fun and learned so much that I took the Level 2 class a year later and got a second PunchLine gig. I am a better public speaker today because of the lessons I learned from Jeff. Google: "Ricky Steele Punchline" to see either of my graduation sets. I strongly suggest you enjoy a 12 pack of PBR or a fifth of tequila before watching and you will find me hilarious. Stone Sober, not so much.

Life is no joke, but I enjoy laughing, and I have seen the medicinal power of laughter work on others, just as Proverbs 17:22 promises. Each of us has issues, whether it be our marriages, issues with our children, health, financial and any number of others. If I can say something that is funny or uplifting and it takes someone's mind off of their pain for just thirty seconds, that thirty seconds may have been the single reason God put me on this earth. Whenever I can make a friend or client going through a rough patch feel good enough to smile or even laugh, that is better than any piece of business I have sold in my entire career.

The Greatest Networkers of Our Time

I do not care if you, your parents, or grandparents voted for Jimmy Carter or if you think he did a good job as our thirty-ninth president. You cannot deny his greatness as a networker. To most folks, Governor Carter's chances of winning the White House appeared as good as a snowball in hell. But it only took one person believing he could win, and that man made it happen. He rang doorbells, especially in the Northeast, but also around the country. His grassroots Peanut Brigade was the very essence of networking. Friends and friends of friends left their homes from all over Georgia to campaign nationally, and you know what was accomplished.

Without doubt, Jimmy Carter has had a greater impact on the world than any other former president in history. I'm not going to catalog all the humanitarian causes President Carter has championed. You can go to the Carter Center website at www.cartercenter.org for a full and accurate accounting. But two initiatives in particular both amaze and touch me: his work in Africa to eradicate the guinea worm, and his work in Africa as well as Latin America to fight river blindness. My wife and I were fortunate to hear President Carter speak at the Carter Center several years ago. Speaking without notes, he covered a dazzling range of subjects. He told of the great success the Carter Center has achieved against the guinea worm and river blindness. He took no credit for himself but talked about the power of his network. It was his network, he said, that had triumphed. Johnson & Johnson, Precision Fabrics, E.I. DuPont, BASF, Hydro Polymers, Merck and Company, Lions Club International, WHO, World Bank, the government of Japan, and the Bill Gates Foundation, all were part of President

Carter's network, working together to solve these pressing world problems.

Mesh to seine the stagnant portions of rivers and streams, vaccine for Africa and Latin America, educational material and instructors to teach prevention techniques, these are just a few of the resources provided by Carter's network. The results? Staggering. The number of cases of guinea worm decreased from 3.5 million in 1986 to fewer than 50,000 in 2010 to just 14 cases in 2021. This horrible disease will be wiped out in the next few years, and it would not have happened if not for President Carter and The Carter Center's work through their network over the last thirty years.

River blindness affects 18 million people in Africa and Latin America. Thanks to Carter's networking, vaccines have been donated, and experts now believe that it is possible to eliminate river blindness in the Western Hemisphere very soon. If they are right, this disease will be only the second in history (smallpox was the first) to be completely eradicated.

An equally powerful modern networker is Andrew Young, Reverend, Ambassador, Mayor, and Humanitarian. I first met Andy Young at his inaugural celebration after he was elected mayor of Atlanta in 1980. In Columbus, Georgia, I had worn a rented tuxedo three times: junior and senior proms and my wedding. I *bought* my first tuxedo in Atlanta for the inauguration, and I am proud to have on my office wall a picture of Mayor Young with my wife, Beth, and me. I watched Mayor Young, an outsider in city politics, absorb a tremendous amount of criticism from his detractors. He never struck back, but, as the consummate servant leader, always turned the other cheek. I only wish I could muster that much love and forgiveness for others.

Mayor Young used his network to make Atlanta a better place to live. Andy opened doors for Atlanta's business community throughout the world through the network he created while he was the United States ambassador to the United Nations and during his humanitarian and ministerial globetrotting over the years. In 1988 or so, a brave visionary Atlanta lawyer had a dream. William Porter Payne was going to bring the 1996 Olympics to our city. Las Vegas bookmakers would never even have posted odds on it happening because most folks thought the very notion was ridiculous. But Billy Payne did remarkable things using his network of hundreds of friends who pulled in hundreds of their friends. Today, in the middle of Centennial Olympic Park, stands a bigger-than-life-size statue of Billy, a hero to our city and a wonderful person. I am confident that Billy and everyone else who worked closely on the Olympic bid would tell you that, without Andrew Young, the Olympic dream would not have become reality. Atlanta was in a race with Athens, Greece, which was the sentimental favorite, since 1996 was the hundredth anniversary of the modern games, first played in Athens. The Atlanta Bid Team, including Billy Payne, met with each of the Olympic committee voting members during the long bid process. I am sure each of the voters were impressed with Billy and the energetic staff of volunteers who catered to their every whim, but, in the end, I believe the final, winning votes were produced through Andy's network.

He built a network of relationships forged as ambassador, statesman, mayor, civil rights leader, and humanitarian, which no other committee member could have built. Andy's relationships were not predicated on a cocktail party or a schmooze event. He built them over many years, and his friendships and network contacts became *the* Olympic swing votes.

I am positive that I will never have the impact of President Carter or Ambassador Young on this planet. But that is okay. I have my family, friends, neighborhood, business associates, and many others I can touch. None of us knows what our impact will be until we actually begin our journey into servanthood. Improve one other life in your community, and you will have lived a significant life yourself, a life that honors both God and your fellow man. Build your network, enjoy the success of your labors, and then reap the wonderful joy that comes only to those who have loved another with no other motive than that love.

One of my current favorite writers and thought leaders I follow is Simon Sinek. Last weekend, he posted on Facebook something that not only excited me, but I knew that I had to find a place in the book to include it because, in reality, this is the heart and foundation that I have been trying to share with you over these 200+ pages.

```
The goal of life
is not to have our lives
mean something to ourselves.

The goal of life
is to have our lives
mean something to others.



                  @simonsinek
```

Epilogue

The Power to Change Lives through Networking

MY GREATEST SUCCESS IN NETWORKING NEVER MADE ME A DIME but it changed my life forever. In 1985, I was honored to be selected as a member of the Leadership Atlanta program, an organization that has been creating leaders in Atlanta since the first class in 1970. For one year, members study the issues facing our city and discuss what can be done about them. Leadership Atlanta was the first program of its kind in the country, and now there are hundreds, including several more in the Atlanta area, such as Leadership Cobb, Leadership Buckhead, and Leadership DeKalb. In our third or fourth monthly program we studied poverty. Our day began by standing in line at St. Luke's Soup Kitchen with the 500 homeless and hungry guests that St. Luke's serves daily.

I was not ignorant about poverty, but I had never been so close to those living in it. After lunch, we heard several presentations by local not-for-profit groups that dealt with poverty issues. I cannot tell you who any of the speakers were or what the subject matter was—except in one instance. Bill Bolling, the founder of St. Luke's Soup Kitchen and also the founder of the Atlanta Community Food Bank, spoke in a way that touched me. I saw in his eyes and heard in his words a love unlike any I had ever witnessed before. I left the program that afternoon and could hardly tell my wife what I had experienced.

As with all too many emotional experiences, life gets in the way, and even before the end of that week, the Poverty Day was no longer top of mind. About a week later, however, I was in the shower thinking about the busy day I had ahead of me. All of a sudden, the Leadership Atlanta Poverty Day overwhelmed me. I could hardly finish my shower. I knew that something had to be done, and I was going to do my best to be involved in doing it.

At that time, I was in the hospitality industry and co-owned the largest independent transportation company in the Atlanta area. We were the exclusive service provider for Hartsfield International Airport (today, Hartsfield-Jackson International Airport), the Georgia World Congress Center, and all of Atlanta's convention hotels. We also had a division that produced special events, everything from a golf tournament to a spouse shopping spree to lavish banquets at the Ritz Carlton, including hiring talent to perform, such as the Atlanta Symphony Orchestra. In our business, we always over-ordered food. As a service business, we knew that 10 percent too much food was better than a 1 percent shortage. As a result, we threw away a lot. I also attended many industry events, which routinely stocked as much as twice the food the attendees were able to eat. It dawned on me that we could create a system to take this excess food and deliver it to the organizations that serve the hungry.

I mulled over the idea for several days before sharing it with a few people. Most of them said that it was a great idea, but they wondered: How could I possibly get it started? And how could it be paid for?

They were both excellent questions. I was fortunate that one of my classmates in Leadership Atlanta was also the current director of St. Luke's Soup Kitchen. I called Andy Loving and told him that I would like to meet to discuss an idea. At our meeting, Andy said that it was not the dumbest idea he had ever heard, and he suggested a second meeting with Bill Bolling of the Atlanta Community Food Bank. We met at Andy's office a few weeks later. Mr. Bolling listened intently and, after my presentation, said that he had tried for years and years to get the hospitality industry involved, but there was no interest. What I lack in brain power, I make up in naiveté. I also have never enjoyed hearing the word *No*. I told Mr. Bolling that I would make a few calls to see if I could stir up the required interest.

My first call was to Ted Sprague, who at that time was the CEO of the Atlanta Convention and Visitors Bureau. As mentioned earlier in this book, I was on Ted's board due to graciousness of Bill Cambre.

Ted expressed interest and suggested that we meet with Bob King, CEO of the Georgia Hotel and Travel Association.

Networking is about taking the resources you have and doing something with them. Relationships that had been created over the past half-dozen years were about to bear fruit. I suggested to Bill that we hold a summit in Atlanta to discuss the idea. Another friend, Horst Schultz, who at that time was president of the Ritz Carlton Hotel Group, gave us a free meeting room along with lots of food and beverage. The irony of meeting in Atlanta's finest hotel with delicious food to discuss how to feed hungry and homeless folks was duly noted by us all. The attendees included the CEOs of the Convention and Visitors Bureau, the Georgia Hotel and Travel Association, the Georgia World Congress Center, and the owners or general managers of every major hotel in the city. The outcome of the summit was a commitment to study the feasibility of the project.

I am not a patient person, and I was ready to send one of my vehicles to pick up food and deliver it that very day. Fortunately, I listened to much smarter and more patient council. We worked for six months putting together the structure, hiring a wonderful person, Rob Johnson, to be the director, securing the blessing of the Health Department for the city of Atlanta, and meeting with the major restaurateurs. In April of 1987, Atlanta's Table picked up the first serving of food from the Fish Market, a very popular and elegant restaurant owned by Pano Karatossis, who at that time owned seven or eight of the city's finest restaurants. I knew Pano from booking his restaurant for our convention groups, and both of us also sat on the boards of the ACVB and GHTA. Every person you meet may become someone who changes our world. If only you put in the effort.

I will never be able to explain in this book or anyplace else the impact Pano has had on Atlanta's Table. He took it upon himself to solicit all of Atlanta's white tablecloth restaurants to participate with him in donating. Pano chaired the Taste of the Nation fund raiser for Atlanta's Table and has raised millions of dollars over the last thirty-four years. In our first year of operation, Atlanta's Table delivered a little over 50,000 pounds of food to agencies that serve the hungry. Today, that number is in the millions of pounds over the last thirty-five years. As a result of our early success, UPS gave us a $5,000,000 grant to create a way to replicate Atlanta's Table across the country. I was then able to use my Meeting Planners International connections to book speaking engagements across the country and Canada where I shared the Atlanta's Table story. A few of the cities used our model and our name to start their own program including Nashville's Table and Seattle's Table, both cities I was able to visit through my network. Atlanta's Table became the model for fresh food distribution to agencies in the US and around the world and at one point, there were more than 150 similar organizations using our model and systems to do the same thing across the globe

Hundreds of Millions of meals have been served—all from a simple idea. In addition, the Atlanta Community Food Bank has leveraged the hospitality industry many times over the years and continues to use the new network that was created for them thirty-five years ago, even today, None of this would have been possible if not for a network that had been created over time. Needless to say, I only mentioned a few of the heroes of Atlanta's Table. Dorothy Beasley, Phil Noyes, Guy Thomson, Jim Thompson, and Marina Bryant are a few more of the hundreds who have contributed to the effort. I'm sorry I can't mention everyone here. You know who you are, and I am confident you know how much you have changed lives.

Outside of my faith and my family, nothing has had more profound effect on my life than taking part in the creation of Atlanta's Table. All the business success and awards I have received pale by comparison to watching this project become real. Bill Bolling became my friend, confidant, and spiritual advisor during the process, and I will be in his debt forever for these reasons and one more. The man I met because of Leadership Atlanta in the Fall of 1985 is the same man who conducted the funeral service for our son, Andrew. The power of networking to better the world is as good a reason as any to learn how to network. You will benefit personally and professionally as you make your contribution to society. You don't have to do something as big as Atlanta's Table, much less something like an Andrew Young or President Carter has done. If you have a positive impact on the life of one senior citizen, child, veteran, or anyone with special needs, *that is heroic and* will be your legacy.

Win Friends, Not Arguments

It is a sad fact that as you become more successful in business, as your network of clients and friends grows, so the ranks of your enemies will multiply. No matter how hard you try to live the Golden Rule, your heightened profile will create jealousy and envy among competitors and even among colleagues. This is not your failure—or, for that matter, theirs. It is a fact of life and of business. But when you find yourself being attacked, you are never forced to return fire. No one wins in these sniping situations, and usually the harder you fight the faster the quicksand of rumor, innuendo, and invective swallows you up. Enemies are inevitable, but people who spend half their lives deliberately making enemies must spend the other half looking over their shoulder. It's not worth it.

"The reason I can't follow the old eye-for-an-eye philosophy is that it ends up leaving everyone blind," Martin Luther King, Jr. said in May 1963. Dr. King lived this philosophy, as did the great missionary Dr. E. Stanley Jones. Publicly slandered on an occasion when he had tried to do a good deed, he was asked about the accusations leveled at him. "The Christian is not in the business of winning arguments, but of winning people," Jones replied.

Whether you are a Christian, worship in another house of faith, or believe in nothing much at all, this is truth for all of us. *We* are not in the business of winning arguments, but of winning friends, creating relationships, and establishing clients. It is much, much easier to do this business if you try to live at peace with everyone. Seek or even obtain revenge, and you win nothing except a life-long involvement in a vicious cycle.

Easier said than done? My lawyer and friend for over forty years,

A. J. Block, gave me this advice years ago when I was, to put it bluntly, shafted by a former employee. I was meeting with Jay, demanding he sue the guilty party, take his house, burn his cars, and do a few other things better left unsaid, all to right the wrong that had been done to me.

"Take out your best stationery," Jay responded. "Write a handwritten letter to the person who is your oppressor. Be very specific in telling them how hurt you are and that you do not believe you deserved their hatred or mistreatment. Tell them the pain they caused you, your family, and your employees. Tell them what you think they deserve as a punishment for their mortal sin. Finish your letter by saying something extremely vulgar about their momma. Reread the letter, seal it, and put a stamp on it. Do nothing else in your life before either shredding or burning the letter. Nothing good will ever come from sending it, and a tremendous amount of additional pain can be guaranteed if you do mail it. Hopefully, writing it and getting ready to mail it will get enough of it off your chest so that your life will actually go on."

Jay's suggestion was a great lesson in the art of forgiveness. Over the years and after too many unpleasant situations, I now fully understand that although my pain may be genuine and the injury real, the failure to forgive hurts no one more than me. Networks need to grow, business to expand, life to move forward. Hold on to spite, withhold forgiveness, and you're a dead man walking.

I hope and pray something I shared will resonate in your heart and mind. There are unlimited opportunities for you in the world of networking. Take just one of the principles and apply it to your life. Do it today. I have made New Year's resolutions that were broken before sundown on the night of January 1. Old habits are hard to break. If you try something you read here for one or two weeks, and you do not see immediate results, I apologize for not writing and communicating the timetables better. Give it a year, and I promise you will begin seeing results. The second year even more results. I believe that, after five years, you will have long forgotten this book because you will be too busy enjoying the life that comes from being successful at networking.

You may even be writing your own book. That's fine. My interest is not in your remembering this book or me. My only interest is in helping you become the person God intended you to become. I will never know what happens, but God does, and that is good enough for me.

My Final Secret and the Principle Everything Else Is Based On

I have one final point I would like to share with you. Perhaps, this should have been the beginning of the book. Every example in this book and everything I try to live by daily is founded in one principle. I occasionally share this secret when I speak publicly. It is fun to watch the faces of the audience when I do. Some of those faces convey disbelief. I understand. Other faces tell me that, although it may work for me, it will not work for them, because their situation is so much different from mine. To both groups of faces, I would like to point out how easy it is to conclude that something will not work if you never try it.

Well, the secret I offer is difficult, it will take time, and you will often fail in executing it. The good news is that it can also become your secret weapon within a minute of hearing or reading about it. You will make a choice to accept the secret or reject it. If you do attempt to implement it in your life, your life will improve today. You will enjoy life in a new way, and the people you work and live with will begin to notice a difference. I cannot promise you will get a new job, make more money, or win the lottery, but I can promise you will die a very rich person. Puff Daddy rapped back in the day that "It's all about the Benjamin's." I prefer what the Eagles' Don Henley sang years earlier: "They don't make hearses with luggage racks." You will not take your automobile, your boat, your house on the lake, your 401K, or even a single dime with you when you depart Planet Earth. It's the truth, believe it or not.

So, my secret?

My secret is my decision to love every person I meet.

I know that sounds farfetched and I may have lost some of you at this point. Maybe that's why I put it at the end of the book. But, please, hang on just another page or two.

You can do it. Love is a choice. You choose whom you are going to love just as you choose what you are going to have for dinner. Love is an emotion you can use for good. I want to make sure you understand. I never said anything about liking everyone I meet. I have a hard time liking any number of folks. Many I meet do not share my beliefs or values. I struggle at times with the actions, politics, language, and attitudes of others. I find it hard to believe I have met everyone in Atlanta who does not know how to count to 10. But there they are, at the supermarket, standing in front of me in the Express Lane. They are hard people to like. I choose to love them.

Do I ever fail? If you have any doubts, I will be happy to give you my home phone number or the cell phone numbers of my children. Beth, Everett, and Rebecca can tell you many stories of my failures. My sisters, Vicki and Susan, and my brother, Robert, can tell you even more. I do know that life is not a sprint. It is a marathon. Regardless, until I can love you just as you are, including whatever I may find unappealing, I am failing in life.

Every time I fall short in my loving responsibilities, I hope I recognize it. If I don't, I hope my wife, children, or maybe even you will point it out to me. I will then have the opportunity to ask for forgiveness from God and whomever I may have offended. Hard? Yes. But it's much harder to live under the pressure of a life without love.

True freedom begins in the heart, and love is the key ingredient. If you could ask Nelson Mandela, Alexander Solzhenitsyn, or any of the thousands of political prisoners jailed in the last century if their freedom was ever lost, I am confident that all of them would say, "It was not." Their love for others allowed them never to surrender their freedom despite their incarceration. Their captors believed freedom could be imprisoned, but then they watched in disbelief as their system of government faded and freedom became real—for millions. In prison, these heroes, loving others, experienced greater freedom and joy than any of us on the outside content to live without thought, automatically, and without love for absolutely everyone.

Acknowledgments

A LOT HAS CHANGED SINCE I WROTE THE FIRST and the second edition of *Heart of Networking* in 2004 and 2010 respectively. The world is a different place. Some of the changes are great and some too terrible to comprehend. My children are all grown and out of the house. We also lost our son, Andrew in 2017. One of the huge blessings is that we now have five amazing grandchildren.

Our oldest, Richard Everett Steele, III graduated from the University of Georgia, served our country as an army officer in Iraq, is a multi-time entrepreneur, and, along with his wife, Ashley, created our youngest grandchild, Lincoln. Our precious Andrew did his best to fight a hard battle with mental illness while exhibiting grace and love to everyone regardless of his pain, and he gave us our oldest grandchild, Sophie. Rebecca matured into one of the most loving and kindest people I have ever known. She is a successful yoga therapist with her own private practice, and she produced three wonderful and kind grandchildren, Zoe, James, and Ella. Each of these family members give me a reason to get up every day with a smile on my face.

Personally. I have transitioned my career into that of Chief Development Officer at several companies, and today, at seventy years of age, I am working for and with two hard-working young men, Kevin Raxter and Matt Fox, at Talent 360 Solutions. We are Atlanta's most passionate boutique staffing agency focused not on how much money we may make, but on the number of people we can over-serve. Our motto is: "We are Passionate about our clients, our candidates, our community and one another."

Because of the success of the first two editions of this book, I now share the lessons in presentation form to companies, university students, and to not-for-profit groups across the country. This has been a great blessing to me. Meeting new people and sharing what I have been fortunate to learn over the years is a joy. The emails and letters I have received from those who have read my book or attended one of my presentations has been very gratifying. It seems that my book and speeches have struck a chord with many people. For that I am humbled.

I have been a chameleon most of my life, absorbing the positive habits of others over the years and making them part of my skin. Truth to tell, I really need to thank several thousand people and devote to them an entire *Book of Acknowledgments*, with a paragraph or two on each person. Had I actually tried to do this, the first book would never have been finished, because there would always be more names to add—many wonderful people who have had an important impact in my life.

Back in 2004 when writing the first edition, I began typing a list of folks I just *had* to thank, but when the list grew to over a hundred and I kept thinking of more, I just *had* to stop. Instead, I am going to thank now, as I did then, just a few people, mostly family, and I trust that when my friends and mentors read this book, they will already know who they are and know how much I love and care for them. I want to thank each of them for making my life what it is and what it will become. May the Lord bless you and keep you. May the Lord make His face to shine upon you and be gracious to you.

I want to thank and honor my Mother and Father, who both died in 2002, within five months of each other. Words cannot express how much I miss them. They would have been proud of me for writing a book. Based on my grades in school, neither of them had reason to believe I could actually read a book, much less write one. My parents were two very special people, and I am who I am because of them. My father taught me 90 percent of everything I know, both the good and the bad. He was the consummate networker before anyone heard or used the term. I grew up watching him accomplish the seemingly impossible by leveraging his relationships with friends and other influential people in our community. He had some great successes and some great failures, but he was the same person in either situation.

I thank God for my father-in-law, Jimmy Ellis, who died many years too early. I learned lessons from Jimmy that my dad did not have the ability to teach. And thus, I am blessed to have had two wonderful fathers as teachers. My mother-in-law, Patsy Ellis, left us shortly before the Second Edition was released, after many years of struggling with illness. I will never be able to repay her for always being there for me, my wife, and our children whenever we called.

Our two surviving children, Everett and Rebecca, continue to give my life joy. I have learned more about honesty, loving, and giving from my children than from a thousand sermons I have heard or books I have read. Each of them is enjoying success and personal satisfaction more than I ever dreamed. I am both proud and honored to be their father.

To my precious Andrew, you may have left this earth on October 10, 2017, but you have never left my heart for five seconds

My wife, Beth, is one of a kind, and I love her much more today than I did in 1979 when we first married. Fine wine has never aged as perfectly as Beth. I never did anything good enough to deserve a wife like her. She certainly never did anything so bad in her life to deserve me. I am thankful to God for putting Beth in my life. She has been behind the scenes in every success I have achieved and helped clean up every mess I created. Without her in my life, I would never have made it through the hard times, and there have been many. Beth opened my eyes to so many truths in the world to which my preconceptions had blinded me. Beth gave me the title for this book after my months of fruitless brainstorming. She is the strength in our family and the primary reason our children are as wonderful as they are.

Bill Bolling and Martin Lehfeldt, have loved on me, scolded me, thought about cursing me (but I am bigger than they are), laughed with me, cried with me, and quite often drank with me when drinking was needed to celebrate or to dull the pain of situations that made life very painful over the past thirty-five years. I love you, Bill and Martin, and my life would not have been as rich, if not for the two of you. I have both of you in my will to be making remarks at my funeral service. I wrote it in ink so you have to outlive me. Don't mess up my plans.

The third person is my friend and editor of all three of these books, Alan Axelrod. Over the last sixteen years, Alan has become a friend, confidant, and sounding board. He is an accomplished author in his own right with more than a hundred books to his credit. I am grateful—and I am sure you are—that Alan was able to take my often-disjointed thoughts and make them readable. You can learn more about Alan at http://en.wikipedia.org/wiki/Alan_Axelrod or by contacting him at adaxelrod@comcast.net. Thank you, Alan.

Finally, this is the last and certainly the most important "Thank You" in this book.

I want to say "Thank You" to you and every other reader of this book. There are thousands and thousands of books written each year and you decided to read mine. It is both humbling and quite inspiring to me. I hope you found this book worth your investment of time and concentration. If you would like to write me any comments—positive, negative, to ask me a question, or for advice—my personal email is ricky@rickysteele.net. Also feel free to post your comments to *The Heart of Networking Third Edition* on Amazon, so others will know what to expect before buying the book for themselves or as a gift.

I wish each of you great success. I believe following the principles of The Golden Rule through becoming a Servant Leader will make you a great success in business and in life.

Micah 6:8:
He has shown you, O mortal, what is good. And what does the Lord require of you? To act justly and to love mercy and to walk humbly with your God.

—Ricky